ANGER WORK

ANGER WORK

How to Express Your Anger and Still Be Kind

Dr. Robert E. Puff, Jr., M.Div., Ph.D.

Edited by Kelly M. Arbor

VANTAGE PRESS
New York

Copyright © 1999 by Dr. Robert E. Puff, Jr., M.Div., Ph.D.

Published by Vantage Press, Inc.
516 West 34th Street, New York, New York 10001

Manufactured in the United States of America
ISBN: 0-533-12956-7

Library of Congress Catalog Card No.: 98-90860

0 9 8 7 6 5 4 3 2 1

To my wife and best friend; her insights have increased my own understanding, and her support has made this book possible

Contents

What is Anger Work?

Anger work is a psychological tool that is used to heal oneself from past and present emotional pains. **The basic premise of Anger Work is to let go of emotionally painful events by focusing on them and expressing anger about the pain. By focusing on the trauma over and over, the pain will gradually go away, never to affect you again.**

A comparison can be made between our physical health and our emotional health. When the body experiences a severe laceration or other injury, if the wound is left unattended, it will get infected. Eventually, it will fester and may even turn into gangrene, a life-threatening condition. If, however, the wound is cleansed thoroughly and allowed to heal completely, all that is left is a scar to remind the victim of the event.

Likewise, when an emotional wound is sustained by the psyche, if it is not addressed, and feelings are repressed, it will fester as surely as any physical wound. As a result it will start to affect other areas of the person's life, just as infection spreads to other parts of the body. Since abusive people and emotional pain are part of everyday life, the person who does not learn to deal appropriately with them will start to experience a cumulative negative effect. Eventually the individual's overall emotional and psychological health will be at risk.

If, however, the emotional wound is cleansed well, and allowed to heal completely, all that is left is a memory. This memory, like an old scar, does not hurt. It becomes no more than a record of your personal history, an experience that you have learned from. Anger Work is the cleansing process that can bring this healing about.

Who Needs Anger Work?

There are three categories of people who can benefit from doing Anger Work. The first category is comprised of people who are already consciously angry and need to find some constructive way of resolving their feelings. The second category consists of those who don't *feel* angry, but who struggle with interpersonal or intrapersonal difficulties and have never fully processed the traumatic events that shaped them and set them up for the problems they face today. The third category includes those individuals who have successfully dealt with all the issues from their past, but are interested in healthy ways of handling aggravating situations that come up in their current, daily lives.

Those Who Know They're Angry

First let me address those of you who know you're angry. You have been mistreated or abused and you've had enough of that. You may be in touch with the feelings of your anger, but you have not yet started expressing them, or you may be a seasoned veteran at "giving people a piece of your mind." You may even have a "temper problem" and experience episodes in which your anger seems to have control of you, rather than your being in control of your anger.

People have been getting angry since the beginning of time: that is nothing new. You may be thinking I don't need a book to tell me to get mad when somebody does something that ticks me off! But Anger Work is not simply "getting mad" at someone, nor does it deal exclusively with the present.

People who describe themselves as having a "temper problem" are generally people who have had some very negative experiences in the past. Because they have not yet successfully worked through all their feelings about these events, they walk around with "leftovers." That is, leftover anger from situations that happened a long time ago.

They bring these "leftovers" with them into every new situation. The result is that they are already somewhat angry before anything happens. So when someone does something that might normally be a minor source of irritation, the person with "leftovers" finds him or herself inordinately angry. They feel the anger of the current situation plus the "leftovers" they had in store. In situations that would normally make them feel genuinely angry, and for good reason, they go beyond that and become explosive. Instead of assertively asking someone to stop the offending behavior, they may haul off and slug the person or berate them verbally.

You may be experiencing problems because of angry outbursts you have had, and now you are dealing with the consequences of your expression. Or maybe you haven't done anything regrettable yet, but you feel like a volcano about to explode and burn everything around you. If either of these descriptions fits you, you will find the section "No Acting Out Anger at Others" particularly helpful. You *can* learn how to channel your anger and aggressive feelings in positive ways. Over time you will work out all your residual feelings of anger so that you have no "leftovers." You will break out of the negative cycle of anger, outburst, guilt, regret, shame, and anger (without becoming a doormat).

People Who Don't Feel Angry But
Have Issues from the Past

Some people don't feel angry because they can't think of anything to feel angry about. Others refrain from feelings of anger because they think anger is bad, or because it frightens them. They may know they have plenty to feel angry about, but they cannot get in touch with their angry feelings for some reason.

First let me address those of you who can't think of anything to feel angry about. You may have had some sad, painful, or frightening experiences in the past that still bother you. You may know that you're not finished healing from them, and even that they still impact your behavior and the choices that you make today. However, when you consider those experiences, anger does not seem like the appropriate response to you. So instead, you try not to let it bother you, and if possible, to learn from the experience. But mostly, you try to move on.

In the following section, "Things People Do Instead of Feeling Angry," I've listed a number of coping mechanisms people use when they have issues that they don't know how to resolve. If you recognize any of the behaviors in yourself, or if you struggle with low self-esteem, then you are suffering needlessly. Anger Work can empower you to work through your issues and take control of your life. The very fact that you are struggling in the way that you are is reason enough to get mad.

You don't even have to be mad at anyone in particular; you can simply be mad about the situation. If you don't yet know how your problem got started, you can do Anger Work focused on obliterating your depression or addiction and rising above it. If you have a hard time getting in touch with your anger, you may want to start exercising. This often helps to bring the anger to the surface as you begin to feel more empowered. In the meantime, you will have the side benefit of getting physically fit. I assure you that you will find plenty of fodder for your Anger Work as you trace your problem to its original source.

Now for those of you who don't get angry because you feel guilty when you get mad. Perhaps you have been taught by your family, teachers, or religious community that it is wrong to get angry, or that it should be a brief phase passed through as quickly as possible on your way to forgiveness. Well, I say that anger is a normal, human emotion. And when managed correctly, it plays an important role in the maintenance of a healthy psyche, body, and spirit.

I agree that forgiveness is an important part of the journey to emotional and spiritual wholeness. However, quick forgiveness is often false forgiveness, and false forgiveness can be detrimental to the health (both mental and physical) of the one who practices it. In that sense, false forgiveness can be worse than no forgiveness.

When someone has hurt you deeply, been unfaithful to you, belittled, raped, terrorized, or abandoned you, you are left with all sorts of emotional baggage to sort through. It is not healthy to simply say, "that's okay" or act as if nothing ever happened. It is *not* okay. You have a right to be mad. Something *did* happen, and you've got to deal with it.

You can rush yourself into professing forgiveness only to discover later that anger is still sweltering inside of you. Then you may feel guilty for having this anger (because you supposedly already forgave that person) and engage in all sorts of behavior to try to make it go away. (See the following section on "Things People Do Instead of Getting Angry.")

One of my clients, Bob, reported to me that he was not angry about anything in his life. He had come to me because he just did not want to feel depressed anymore. After a few sessions with Bob, I met with his wife, Karen. I learned that Bob loved to tease Karen. She had had an affair two years earlier and Bob had immediately forgiven her. But shortly thereafter, his teasing of Karen increased and he got depressed.

6

I encouraged Bob not to tease his wife and instead to do Anger Work about the affair. Although he did not feel angry at first, the anger soon came out, for it had been lying just under the surface the whole time. It was his unresolved anger that had been motivating his jabs to Karen. He felt good about doing his Anger Work because it made it easier for him to stop teasing Karen. He did not want to shame or hurt his wife anymore. Bob's depression gradually went away, and their marriage grew closer because he finally got rid of the resentment that he had been harboring for so long.

We tend to deal with things the way we were taught to deal with them. Sometimes this teaching comes in the form of overt statements from our role model, such as "don't be mad," "you have no right to get angry at me," or "let bygones be bygones." "Forgive and forget" is another classic favorite. But often the most powerful message is a simple attitude, which is learned by example from parents who never express anger themselves. Now that you are grown up, and responsible for your own life, it is time to reevaluate the teachings that your family may have passed on to you and make a conscious choice about how you want to handle things.

In Bob's case, his family had always been big teasers while he was growing up. His mom would tease his dad about drinking too much beer, and his dad would tease his mom about getting fat. No one ever talked openly about what was bothering them. Bob fell into the same pattern without even realizing it. Once he became aware of how destructive his behavior was (eroding Karen's self-esteem while adding to his own depression), he chose to stop teasing and vent his anger in the form of Anger Work instead.

There is nothing wrong with feeling angry, even for a long time, when someone hurts you deeply. Anger is a natural, healthy response to abuse. Still, it is not a good enough reason to become abusive yourself. Your anger is there for a reason. Learn to make it your friend. It can help you retrace your steps through the valley of the shadow of death (for isn't that what life's most painful and frightening experiences are?) You will come out on the other side liberated from the grip of the past. Anger Work can serve as a path on your journey to wholeness, and forgiveness of yourself and others is part of what you may find along the way.

Maybe you don't feel guilty at the idea of getting angry; the whole thing simply frightens you. As far as you're concerned, anger is scary stuff. Maybe you decided never to get angry because you lived with someone who constantly ranted and raged, inflicted anger on all who was near. As a result you have become just as extreme in refraining from anger as the rager was in expressing it. I often hear people talking as though if you really got into expressing your anger, it would send you "over the deep end" and you'd lose control. This has never been my experience in working with people, as long as they follow the two rules that are the Essential Keys to Successful Anger Work described later in this book.

Years ago I worked with an older gentleman who had been in the Korean War and had repressed his anger about his war experiences for many years. He was convinced that if he ever let his anger out, something terrible would happen. I assured him that expressing his anger would be very beneficial for him, and arranged for him to get a soft bat and a bed mattress so that he could do Anger Work. We went to a prearranged room where he was free to let out his anger while I held up the mattress.

I must admit that I was a little nervous because he had talked in such detail about how his anger could destroy the whole hospital, let alone the mattress that I would be holding! I was glad to learn that his anger did not live up to his expectations. He did hit the bed hard, but he could only hit repeatedly for less than a minute. Instead of his anger destroying everything in sight, he found that the room, and even the bat, were virtually unaffected by his display of wrath. However, he did discover that he felt much less agitated after our session.

It has always been my experience that as long as anger is directed at objects and not people, no one will be harmed. Of course, don't go out and destroy a person's car or house, or item of sentimental value. This will hurt them indirectly. You do not want to hurt anyone with your anger, directly or indirectly.

You may have identified some specific experiences in your life as traumatic (such as physical, sexual, or emotional abuse, a bad marriage, loss of a loved one, or loss of physical capability due to injury, etc.) Yet still, you have never fully processed those experiences or been angry about the pain you went through. Holding on to one's anger is what begins the progression toward more and more serious problems like those mentioned in the section "Consequences of Not Doing Anger Work."

It's time to start cleaning those wounds so you can heal properly. If you follow the guidelines in this book, you will be able to process your pain and work your way out of the victim role without raging uncontrollably, frightening yourself and others. Anger Work is especially effective for those trying to grow out of living life as a victim. Allowing yourself to feel angry over the abuse that you have sustained in the past is a very empowering experience. You will find yourself less and less willing to be victimized again. Instead, you will respond with appropriate anger when people attempt to take advantage of you. However, if you choose not to address your unresolved issues, you will find yourself stuck with the people described in the section "Things People Do Instead of Feeling Angry."

Those Who Have No Past Issues, But Want to Live to the Fullest

Perhaps you do not have recollection of any particularly disturbing events from your past. You may have had a very happy childhood, and not yet been in a relationship or situation that left you reeling. If you do not have any of the problems listed under the following section, "Things People Do Instead of Feeling Angry," then it is possible that you are one of those rare and fortunate individuals who honestly has no big issues from your past to deal with.

Nevertheless you are still faced with the challenge of how to deal with the difficult people and aggravating situations of current everyday life. We all encounter people at various times in our lives who would like to control us, hinder our progress in some area, or who simply act like jerks. We all have to deal with interpersonal conflict and face failure in various endeavors.

Anger Work is a practical tool for processing the feelings these situations create. By doing Anger Work, you can flush out the negative energy generated by them. At the same time, you are reducing your stress and increasing your energy level. You will find that you are able to solve interpersonal problems more quickly and you will spend less time trying to take back words that you said in the heat of an argument. **I recommend Anger Work to anyone and everyone. It is simply a healthy way to process the negative experiences of life, from severe traumas to minor irritations.**

Once you have learned how to use Anger Work to process your feelings about the negative experiences of life, this ability can serve as a great asset to you. Every life contains a measure of suffering. Perhaps nothing tragic has happened to you thus far, but eventually, if nothing else, someone you love will become sick and die. When this happens you will have the tools to deal with your loss.

Things People Do Instead
of Feeling Angry

Many people have troubling thoughts that return to them whenever they slow down enough to have quiet time to think. You probably know someone who will tell you he doesn't like to be alone, or a friend who says she likes to keep busy because otherwise she "thinks too much." In actuality, of course, the mere quantity of thoughts is not the problem . . . surely everyone can afford a free hour or two of thought each week without any harmful effects. Yet many busy people do not allow even that much time for quiet contemplation. The reason is that they find their thoughts continually returning to particular memories, worries, feelings of guilt, or self-doubt.

Usually people feel helpless with respect to making the memories go away, solving the problem, or resolving the nagging feelings. The best they can do is to avoid these recurring thoughts by not allowing themselves time to think. They find some behavior or substance that is the emotional equivalent of a painkiller (a drug that deadens the sensation of pain without remedying the source of the pain). They may turn to a variety of means for suppressing their feelings.

Some people turn to drugs (prescription or illicit) and alcohol to alter their moods so that they don't have to feel their true responses to the events of their life. This is the most well-known type of addiction, but there are other ways to suppress your feelings that don't involve substance abuse, and these may be harder to recognize. Unlike the decision to take a pill when you've got a headache, the decision to suppress feelings is not always a conscious choice. Some addictions are so subtle that they are even socially acceptable.

For example, one method is to develop a sort of addiction to romance. People who choose this route may constantly keep finding new love interests to occupy their time and/or thoughts. This may take the form of short, serial relationships with a pattern of breaking up or moving on as soon as it gets "boring." In this case, "boring" usually means that the initial "getting to know you" or infatuation stage has passed.

There is another form of this "romance addiction" in which the individual may have long-term, rocky relationships. The partners may fight passionately, make up, and then love passionately, only to start the cycle over again. Whenever things start to calm down, one of the partners will introduce some new, troubling behavior to ensure that things remain consistently tumultuous. Regardless, the two feel inexplicably drawn to one another. For both types of romance addicts, an ordinary, long-term relationship with a stable partner will not do, because such a relationship is not consuming enough to serve its purpose. It is deemed "boring" because it does not provide adequate distraction from whatever they are running from.

Another addiction that may overlap with romance addiction, though not usually, is sexual addiction. In this case addicts obsess over the idea of engaging in sexual activity. Depending on the severity or mildness of the case, this behavior can sometimes be viewed as socially acceptable. It can range from monogamous relationships in which the sexual aspect is overemphasized, to extremely perverse behavior. Other examples include bar-hopping and one-night stands, married partners who are habitually unfaithful, pornography addicts, and child abusers.

Sex addicts may devote enormous amounts of time to the pursuit of partners, or to fantasizing and self-stimulation. Their encounters are not characterized by genuine emotional intimacy, because genuine intimacy requires that both partners be in touch with their feelings. Sex addicts use sex to hide their real feelings. They are not emotionally available to the partner if there is one, and they may even be overtly abusive.

Work addiction or "workaholism" is one of the most socially acceptable addictions that there is. In fact, unlike most addictions, this one can even generate praise and admiration for the addict. Many work addicts are financially successful and hold prestigious positions. The line between healthy ambition and work-addiction is often fuzzy. Anyone who works for salary knows that there is always something else you could stay late to work on. Those who punch a time clock can sign up for overtime or get a second or third job. Often these extra jobs seem necessary just to "make the bills." Remember, most bills represent choices made. What are you choosing above your own peace and wholeness? Power-locks and windows on your car? More toys? Think about it.

If you keep your mind so focused on your work that it precludes having time to feel or think about your problems, worries, and doubts, then you are probably addicted to your work. However, workaholism is not the only way to accomplish this effect. There is another category of addiction that I call "busyism."

Busyism is very close to work addiction. The main difference is that you do not get paid for your efforts, and your time and energies can be spread over a broader spectrum of interests. Like work addiction, busyism is likely to bring you praise from the outside world for your devotion and many hours of service.

An example of busyism is the college student who takes eighteen units, is vice-president of the Honor Society, actively participates in a political action group, mentors an at-risk youth, and is present for all family functions. There never seems to be enough time to resolve those nagging doubts or ask the big questions.

Another example is the "stay-at-home" mom who never seems to have any time to stay at home because she is always taking her kids, the dry-cleaning, the Cub Scouts, or her father who is in failing health somewhere. She often feels frazzled and never has time for herself.

Still another example is the business executive who finally retired from his high-stress job only to find himself chairman of the homeowners grounds committee, deacon at his local church, fund-raiser for the new YMCA senior center, and Mr. Fix-it for all his family and close neighbors. He still doesn't have much time for dates with his wife, quiet times of contemplation, or those rambling vacations that he was looking forward to for all those years.

Some people habitually take on "project friends." These friends are very needy and so the "busy" person spends a great deal of time counseling, consoling, and rescuing the project friend from messes s/he has gotten him/herself into. Constantly being involved in someone else's life that is *so* messed up can be very distracting from the problem of one's own life. This is another form of busyism.

Am I saying that everyone who volunteers for a non-profit organization or holds down a good job is somehow off-balance? Of course not! Obviously there is a healthy place for helping others just as there is for work, romance, and sex. It is when you do not balance them with reflective time spent processing your feelings that there is danger. When these activities are habitually used as a means to distract you from the issues that you need to deal with, then you know that you are addicted.

You need to evaluate how much time you have to yourself to reflect on how you're doing, what you're feeling, and whether you have any problems you need to resolve. Are the relationships in your life going well? Are you giving enough time and energy to them? Do you spend the time and energy building into yourself so that if you lost your job or role tomorrow it wouldn't take your identity with it?

Everyone needs some quiet time like this. If you realize that you have none, then I urge you to experiment with taking at least a half a day to be by yourself, examining your feeling about your life, and see what comes up. Remember, anything that may surface is actually there all the time buzzing around in the back of your mind, adding to your stress.

Using the addictions and behaviors just discussed to avoid the deeper issues may help you hold it together and keep up appearances for a while. However, it is as unwise as letting termites eat away at your home. After a while there will be nothing but a shell, and eventually the whole thing will come crashing down around you. Turning to these distractions is like feeling safe only when your head is under the covers. Anger Work provides a means by which you can confront that boogie man lurking in the corner of your mind, and eventually vanquish it.

If you have examined yourself and decided that you do not have any of the addictions listed above, then look a little further and ask yourself if you suffer from depression or stress-related illnesses. These are different from addictions, but they still fall under the category of "Things People Do Instead of Doing Anger Work." Like addictions they serve the roll of distracting you from your true feelings. They are evidence of suppressed emotions.

If you struggle with depression, stress-related illness, or find that you need to use constant activity, alcohol, or other drugs to keep disturbing fears, worries, or self-doubts at bay, these are indicators that you have unresolved issues. They are not going to go away until you find a way to deal with them directly. Applying the skills explained in this book to your daily lifestyle can start you on a journey of healing that will lead you to a place of emotional freedom you've never known before.

Learning from Children

I am a clinical psychologist licensed to work with adults and children who have emotional problems. In the course of my training and work, I have specialized in working with children who are emotionally traumatized, even those as young as two years old. When I work with young children, I allow as much freedom and self-direction in the session as possible. This unstructured environment allows the child to explore his or her emotional pain, express it in play, and be healed.

Many of my insights into the benefits of Anger Work have come from working with children. Children, on the whole, take much less time in therapy to heal from their emotional wounds than adults do. This gives us reason to take a closer look at what children do to heal and to learn from their intuitive wisdom. Children have much to teach us about the natural course of healing. Here are some of the lessons I have learned from kids.

In the fifteen years that I have been working with clients, I have seen children who have experienced a wide range of traumas, like sexual abuse, death of a loved one, divorce, moving to a new neighborhood, or being teased at daycare. As surprising as it may be, I have observed that there are only two emotions that children express to help themselves heal. These two emotions are ANGER and SADNESS.

In affirmation of the wisdom of this natural choice by my young clients, I have noted a similar pattern among my adult clients. Those who make the most progress are those who get in touch with these primary emotions of sadness and anger. As adults we develop other defenses, such as depression, anxiety, phobias, worry, stress-induced illnesses, and a myriad of other non-healing ways of trying to cope with emotional pain. Most adults are willing to try just about anything before grappling with their own raw feelings of anger and sadness. But these two emotions are the true, underlying, instinctual responses we all have to victimization and loss. **Lesson number one from the children: in order to heal, we need to go back to the simple pure emotions of anger and sadness.**

When children are traumatized, they heal from it naturally as long as they are in an environment where it is safe to do so, by expressing their anger or sadness about the pain. Children tend to express and not repress their emotions. Babies, of course, are the prime example of this, crying freely whenever they feel like it. Repression is a learned response. It is only as we grow older that we learn to suppress our feelings.

Now occasionally the ability to repress your feelings can be helpful. For instance, it sometimes comes in handy to repress your response of disappointment to a situation long enough to be able to get home and have a good cry or do Anger Work in a safe environment. However, most adults take repression too far. In contrast with children, some adults *never* cry or display anger. This is unhealthy and we need to learn **lesson number two from the children: Express your feelings, don't repress them.**

The following cases of Shawn and Jamie are good examples of how children use their sadness and anger to heal themselves. (Please note, throughout this book, client names and details have been changed in order to protect the confidentiality of my clients.)

While I was in graduate school, I directed a child-care center. A two-year-old girl named Shawn was left in my care by her parents. It was the first time in her life she had ever been separated from them. The child-care center was open for only three hours a day, on Mondays, Wednesdays, and Fridays, to give graduate students with young children a respite. As I took Shawn from her anxious parents, she immediately started crying. I held her, switching her back and forth between my arms so that I could work with the other children. Shawn cried off and on for the entire three hours. She never did let go of me though I tried to set her down a couple of times. By the time her parents returned, my shirt was soaked.

The next week, Shawn returned and of course started crying the second that her parents left. I held Shawn for about five minutes, and then she stopped crying. After watching the other children playing all around us, she slowly made her way out of my arms. Though she kept a watchful eye out for me a few minutes to make sure that I would rescue her, Shawn began to play. She never cried again when her parents left her at childcare with me. Shawn's tears of sadness helped her heal from the emotional trauma of separation from her parents for the first time in her life.

As the case of Shawn demonstrates, experiencing and expressing your sadness through tears can be an effective tool for healing. However, I find that children between the ages of two and seven primarily express one feeling during their treatment: that is **anger.** They rarely cry about their traumas, they just get angry, sometimes very angry. Afterward they leave the session feeling better, and over time the symptoms that brought them into therapy go away. Children like Jamie in the following story have taught me that expressed anger heals.

Jamie was a two-and-a-half-year-old girl with whom I worked for a year. She was brought to therapy because she had been sexually abused by a man and woman at a day-care center where she was being watched for a few hours. Evidence of this crime was her radical behavior change after the incident. She regressed to soiling her panties, began playing with her private parts, started pinching and biting her younger brother, and did not want to return to the daycare. When I saw her, she appeared to be a sweet little girl who just wanted to play. During all the sessions with Jamie, her mom or dad stayed with us in the same room, reading magazines or books, so that Jamie would give me her full attention.

Quickly Jamie began displaying intense anger towards toys as she played with them. She would growl at them, hit them, throw them, and even try to destroy them. Jamie had told her parents what happened at the daycare, but she never verbalized anything about the abuse during therapy. Her play clearly displayed that she was angry at the abusers who had fondled her private parts. The parents were instructed not to let Jamie aim her anger at them or her younger brother. Gradually during the year, Jamie's behavior improved until she was back to her old self. Therapy was terminated and Jamie has never returned. She is reported to be doing fine.

Jamie had a severe trauma, came into therapy where she could freely express her anger, and got well (went back to her normal developmental process). She was never anxious, depressed, worried, or had any of the myriad of other pseudo-emotions that adults experience. (By pseudo, I mean emotions that we often layer on top to suppress either sadness or anger.) She was simply angry.

Another observation I have made while working with hundreds of children, some of them for years, is that they need to express their anger at inanimate objects, and not at their peers or their family. The more they follow this guideline, the more emotionally healthy they become. If they direct their anger inappropriately by becoming abusive to others, the expression of anger does not have the same healing effect for them. Instead they simply create additional problems for themselves. If they consistently lash out at others in a school setting, they are called bullies. Bullies are not happy. Let me share another example that may help to illustrate this point.

Tony was an eight-year-old bully. He was always getting in trouble at school for teasing and tripping younger kids. At home he would go into his younger sister Kelsey's room, take her Barbie doll, and hide it in the back yard. Other times, he would take strings that had bells or forks attached to them and tie them to the cat's tail in order to torment the poor old cat.

Once Sam, the family's golden retriever who loved table food, had to be rushed to the animal emergency hospital because he had suddenly become deathly ill. After surgery, the veterinarian found a cactus spine in Sam's stomach. Tony confessed that he had given the cactus spine to Sam covered in butter.

His parents were very concerned and did not know what to do. First I helped them to come up with rewards for when Tony was behaving properly and use time out for when he was taking out his anger on others. Time out is a discipline technique in which the only punishment is lack of stimuli or boredom. This might mean standing or sitting in the corner for a period of five to twenty minutes without interacting with any person or object. Having his parents reinforce appropriate behavior at home, in addition to bringing him to therapy, was very helpful.

Very shortly, Tony began to love coming to therapy, because here he and I had lots of toys and he could do whatever he wanted. He was free to express his anger, as long as he did not direct it at me. His favorite "toy" was my couch. He loved to throw things at it, jump on it, hit it with bats, etc. Unfortunately, he was a strong eight-year-old and I had to replace the couch when therapy ended. But therapy did end and his bullying behavior had ceased.

When Tony first came to see me, his anger was a constant threat, boiling just beneath the surface. He was expressing his anger *at* people and animals, and his problems only snowballed. His self-esteem was very low and he felt that nobody really liked him. He was ostracized on the playground because he had done so many mean things to his classmates that most of them stayed away from him out of self-protection.

In therapy he expressed his anger by directing it at inanimate objects and his life began to transform. He was now releasing his anger regularly, instead of letting it build up. Without all that repressed anger, he didn't feel as many impulses to do mean things. He started playing appropriately with his peers, made some new friends, and began feeling much better about himself.

There was no magic in Tony's treatment, only a free expression of his anger directed at inanimate objects. This simple method of healing works just as well for adults. **Lesson number three from the children: Having an appropriate object for your wrath is essential to your recovery; acting out on people will only take you backwards.**

Another point on which we can learn from children is their natural propensity toward physical activity. The medical profession is constantly emphasizing the need for regular exercise; children are naturally active. Kids are always wiggling or running about, playing games of tag or soccer. In fact, teacher friends of mine tell me that it is not uncommon to see a young child running all around the playground during recess with no apparent direction, flapping her arms, screaming or making noises that are strange (to adult ears). If the child is questioned about this behavior, she will inevitably give a sheepish grin and say that it was nothing.

Imagine how you would feel if it were socially acceptable for you to take a break from your home or work place or three times a day as needed, and work off your stress in a similar fashion! How cathartic that would be! Well, I don't recommend that line of action; however, doing Anger Work can give you that same kind of release.

If you think about it from a historical perspective, it has not been long since our world was much more physically active, like our children's world. In the past, people did more physically demanding work for a living. They spent five to twelve hours a day doing something physical, like chopping wood, harvesting fields, hand-washing the laundry, or grinding grain. This type of work provided more natural opportunities for letting off steam.

Today our lives are often more sedentary. We need to be pro-active in creating opportunities for exercise and include a healthy expression of anger at the same time. My young clients are almost always throwing, shooting, or hitting something during their sessions. In reading this book, you will see how often I combine physical activity with Anger Work. It is not only good for the body, but for the psyche as well.

There are other ways of doing Anger Work, but our bodies are meant to be active, not sedentary. By coupling Anger Work with physical activity, we address both the psychological and physiological affects of stress. Physical activity promotes overall health and is one of the best means of doing Anger Work. **Lesson number four from the children: Stay active and use your body to express yourself, especially when you're doing Anger Work.**

Anger and Sadness

As I mentioned in the section "Learning from Children," there are two emotions that can be utilized in the process of healing from trauma: anger and sadness. Sadness can be a very effective vehicle for healing. The only problem with sadness is that it is such a short leap from there to depression. **Sadness heals; depressions does not.**

Depression can keep a person stuck in the same place for years without any progress. You must be very careful not to fall into depression. Unfortunately, many people find the difference between sadness and depression obscure at best, and they often vacillate between the two. I encourage you to be very careful of depression because this thought disorder has an addictive quality to it. Depression actually keeps a person from getting better and can be a defense against real feelings.

True sadness comes when you reflect on the negative event, cry, and grieve over what happened. Afterward you feel a little bit better. **Each time you feel sadness, you are one step closer to being well.** Real sadness heals.

Depression on the other hand, occurs when you get into a downward spiral of negative thinking. It is wallowing in feelings of hopelessness. Depression only hurts and destroys. **After an episode of depression, you do not feel any better.** It does not cleanse you. In fact you are likely to feel worse because of decisions you made while you were depressed.

It usually starts with one's dwelling on the event, but soon goes beyond sadness about what happened and begins to color your attitude in a broader sense. Depression is characterized by negative self-talk, including guilt-laden and hopeless messages. For example you may tell yourself "X" happened because "I'm so stupid" or keep repeating inside your head "It's all my fault." Whether it is or not, that is not going to heal you.

You may even start assigning significance to the event beyond its appropriate scope. For example, telling yourself "I will never be happy again" or "I don't deserve to be happy," because of the failure of a particular relationship or effort to reach a goal. Or maybe your self-talk takes a less personal tone, such as "The world sucks! People are cruel! You can't trust anyone! Life is meaningless," or "I want to die!"

An example of healthier self-talk would be: "Oh! This hurts so bad! I really messed up. I hate it when I mess up." (Then do Anger Work) and tell yourself "I am going to make *real* sure *this* doesn't happen again, because I don't like the way this feels." If your pain is caused by something out of your control, then you can tell yourself, "This too shall pass, and I will survive somehow, and someday things will look better again." In the meantime, do your Anger Work to keep from falling into depression.

Let me give a couple of examples to illustrate the difference between sadness and depression:

An Example of Healing Sadness

When I was in graduate school, I purchased a beautiful Himalayan kitten from a man who advertised in the local newspaper. Because the owner did not have any papers on him, he was inexpensive and I was thankful. I named my kitten Tibet, and we quickly fell in love. The first night, when he came home, he had so many fleas that I had to give him three baths in order to kill them. Tibet was so traumatized that he spent the whole night sleeping on my neck to feel safe. I had a major exam coming up the next day, but I could not sleep a wink.

We became great buddies and spent immeasurable amounts of time together studying. Tibet would always sit on my book or papers as I worked. He was a member of my family for two years. He and I even had a special song: we would dance to it every time it was played on the radio.

Then one day I came home and Tibet was walking very strangely. I could tell that he was not well. I rushed him to the vet, but he died that evening from feline leukemia. He had contracted the disease before he ever came home with me. I was both very sad and very angry. I thought about Tibet often during the day, and whenever our song came on the radio, I cried during the entire song. Slowly, I began to heal. Because of my intense love for Tibet, two years passed before I was finished grieving and could think of him without crying. I never forgot Tibet, but I did heal.

An Example of Depression

A patient of mine named Kim had lost her six-month-old baby, Kyle to Sudden Infant Death Syndrome (S.I.D.S.). It had been four years since Kyle died, and Kim could not get over the loss because she blamed herself. She kept telling herself that if she had only checked on Kyle, instead of talking on the phone with her friend, he wouldn't have died.

Kim believed that her entire life would be one of misery because of Kyle's death. Her feelings of guilt drove her to depression, and she saw no means of healing. Instead of being sad and grieving over the death of Kyle, she blamed herself over an over for his death. She had developed the habit of calling herself "murderer" and "killer" every time she made even a small mistake, like forgetting to water the plants.

This anger turned inward and left her depressed. She was

punishing herself with abusive self-talk and was beginning to entertain thoughts of suicide. She was caught in a vicious cycle of depression, which was driving her further and further away from life and from her husband. That is when her husband intervened and brought Kim to my office.

When Kim came to me, I helped her realize that her self-hatred was only fueling her depression and was in no way healing her from her loss. Together we decided that her self-hatred and verbal abuse, which she was often not even aware of because the self-talk had become so automatic, needed to stop. She agreed to feel angry at God for taking her baby and stop blaming herself. She did Anger Work over her loss.

She also visited Kyle's grave and talked to him about how much she missed him. This, of course, brought tears of sadness, which helped Kim feel better, unlike her depression, which had only made her feel worse. Slowly Kim healed from the loss of Kyle and was able to forgive herself and God for his death. Now Kim and her husband have two more children and she is happy. She still thinks of Kyle from time to time, as I encouraged her to do after she finished therapy, but her depression is gone and her sadness only lasts while she is thinking of Kyle.

I repeat that I recommend Anger Work over sadness, for the bulk of your healing work. Certain situations, like Kim's, lend themselves to sadness more than others. In these cases letting the tears flow is an important part of the healing process. However, if the sadness starts to become overwhelming, it is time to get mad again. Anger Work empowers you to stay out of depression.

Let me share another example of someone I knew who found healing by getting in touch with his own anger and doing Anger Work. A number of years ago, I had a client named James whose wife Sally was killed instantly when she was hit by a drunk driver. The couple had been married for two years and had not planned on having children for a few more years. This left James all alone. The loss was devastating.

Common psychological knowledge would predict that if James expresses his grief, he should recover from this loss in about two years. But James, like most people in this culture, avoided his pain. Instead of being sad and angry over the loss of his wife, he avoided his feelings.

When James was a child, his father worked long hours at his grocery store business. James remembers when his father's mother died. Dad stayed at work extra late into the evening, because just after Grandma died, he decided to expand the store. James never saw his father cry about the loss. Dad just got busier and was at home less.

Now James was faced with a similar crisis. He was a mail carrier and had a passing interest in several sports. With the death of his wife, James joined the local adult soccer league and started to coach in a junior soccer league as well. Whenever he felt sad or angry about the death of his wife, he controlled his anger by going to more practices and volunteering for extra duties with his junior soccer league team. James's friends were amazed at how little the loss of his wife had influenced him. Within a year James had remarried and maintained all his activities.

Of course, slowly yet perceptibly, James's life was going downhill. He started to have severe headaches, then he struggled with insomnia. He focused on his physical problems from a symptomatic point of view, using alcohol and then medication to keep his insomnia under control. Eventually he had to go on blood pressure medication as well. His health was in definite decline. Overall he felt depressed unless he was very busy. His new marriage was going very poorly. James's wife and children complained that he was often angry and that he had no time for anyone at home. They mostly tried to avoid him.

James's reaction is very typical. Like so many others, he chose to avoid painful memories. But when you do this, the effects of the emotional trauma do not leave. Instead, symptoms of the repressed emotions manifest themselves in a myriad of ways. Drug addictions, poor health, mental disorders, and isolation are just a few of the effects of repression. While it is true that not all problems people go through are caused by repressed feelings, all repressed emotions cause problems. They can haunt people all their lives unless they feel the pain and go through the healing process.

Fortunately, for James, he became so frustrated with all the side effects of his repressed emotions that he decided to try something else. That something else was a phone call to me. He had heard of me through a friend at work and was desperate to try something to help him with all of his "physical problems."

James was a pleasure to work with because he liked to be active. After taking a careful history of his life. I encouraged him to be angry over some of the losses in his life when he played soccer. James was skeptical but willing to try. He came up with the idea of putting a soccer ball in front of a net and kicking the ball over and over.

I encouraged him to be angry about the death of his wife, whom he discovered he still missed and loved. James was angry at God for not protecting his wife and enraged at the drunk driver who killed his wife. James did the therapy assignments that I gave him very religiously; he was motivated to stop coming to therapy as soon as he could because of the cost.

As a therapist I try to use my client's emotional defenses and lifelong habits as an asset. In James's case, he was a very disciplined person who had controlled his emotions by keeping busy. I encouraged him to set aside a certain amount of time each day to do his exercising Anger Work. The length of these sessions was slowly increased over time. James's self-discipline proved to be quite helpful for him.

To the surprise of his wife, his children, and himself, James got better. He enjoyed doing the Anger Work because he always felt so much better afterwards. He did not feel as driven to constant business and started deepening his love for his wife and children. His headaches went away, he slept better, his depression subsided, and to the relief of his doctor, his blood pressure even went down.

Today, James is doing well, and I get updates from him fairly regularly to let me know how he is doing. Sometimes he will come in for a question or two that he has about raising his children or family issues. He still works out regularly and enjoys kicking the soccer ball when he gets angry over something.

With Anger Work the road to healing is so clear. All tragic events in life, whether large or small, may be overcome and healed by simply reflecting on the negative event, releasing anger, and continuing the Anger Work until the event holds no emotional power. Only then can you be truly free. It is such a simple solution for so many people.

Two Essential Keys to Successful Anger Work

Okay, now that we've talked extensively about why Anger Work is a good tool to use in your healing, let's talk about how to do successful Anger Work, and how not to. There are two essential keys to making your Anger Work productive. These are:

1. Do not take out or "act-out" your anger on yourself.
2. Do not act out your anger on others (this includes animals).

Part of the definition of Anger Work is that it does NOT involve acting-out your anger at others or self. So if you're doing that, you're not doing Anger Work, you're just getting mad. But even when you're not in the midst of an Anger Work session, it's important to observe these two principles all day, every day to the best of your ability. If you do, you will find that your Anger Work sessions are very productive. You will see definite progress because you will be working through your existing issues and avoiding creating new issues. If you do not follow these principles, it will inhibit your progress greatly.

Perhaps this analogy will help you. Think of all the negative experiences you need to heal from, such as abuses, losses, and failures, as being a pond that you have to empty in order for the grass to grow there. For some people it's more like a puddle or a lake, depending on the amount and severity of the emotional wounds.

But regardless of how much water there is to bail out, the principle works the same for everyone.

Every time you do Anger Work, it is like bailing water out of that pond. Every time you act-out your anger on yourself or others, you are adding to the amount of water in the pond. As you can see, doing Anger Work is beneficial in any case, if only to keep things from getting too much worse; however, if you really want to see the benefits, you've got to stop letting more water get into the pond.

I had been in practice for a number of years before I realized how critical these two points were. I recommended Anger Work to all of my clients, but the results varied. Everyone benefited to some degree, but some clients would heal at a very fast rate while others would improve much more slowly. I came to realize that there was a pattern. The more closely the person followed these two principles, the more quickly he or she got better. Doing "work" means that you are taking steps toward a goal. If you ignore either of these principles, then you are not doing Anger Work as I recommend, you are simply getting angry. Rather than taking steps toward your goal of wholeness, you may be taking a step back. I cannot overemphasize how critical it is that you learn to follow these two guidelines.

Key #1: No Taking Out Your Anger on Yourself

The first essential key to successful Anger Work is that you don't take-out your anger at yourself through words or actions. Many people get very angry at themselves when they make a mistake or do something wrong. They are tempted to pound on themselves, starve or stuff themselves, engage in demeaning sexual encounters, endanger their lives by unsafe driving, or even mutilate themselves. Others are satisfied with a barrage of insults and negative statements about themselves and their lives. They tell themselves how horrible they are and how hopeless their situation is. This behavior has no place in a lifestyle of health. You must learn to replace this behavior with Anger Work and self-forgiveness.

Learning not to be self-abusive is one of the most challenging parts of the journey to wholeness. The full brunt of your anger should never be directed at yourself. This is not to say that you can't feel angry at yourself. Getting angry with yourself is probably unavoidable, but just as you can feel angry at someone you love without blasting them, likewise you can feel angry at yourself without being mean to yourself.

Why is this point so crucial? Because the worse you treat yourself, the worse you become. The more you tell yourself you are thoughtless, stupid, mean, wicked, etc., the more you become so. The more you tell yourself that you'll never learn or change, the more true that statement becomes. This is what we call a self-fulfilling prophecy. You know that abusing and berating a child is not the best way to raise her to become a healthy, well-adjusted adult. So why would you expect that method to be any more fruitful in dealing with yourself?

Self-abuse will cause Guilt (the realization that WHAT YOU DID was bad) to turn into Shame (the feeling that YOU are bad). Guilt is the natural response of your inner self, putting up a flag to let you know there's a problem. Where you take it from there is your own choice. You can choose to tell yourself that you are bad, and walk around feeling like the scum of the earth, or you can take the difficult step of forgiving yourself and move on.

Many of you may be in total disagreement that shame is bad. After all, people should feel remorse when they hurt another. I agree on that point. The moment of recognition when a person realizes that he or she has done something wrong and wishes he had not is healthy guilt. Its purpose is to motivate us to stop the offending behavior, make amends, and avoid a repeat in the future.

The painful experience of guilt serves much the same function as the physical pain of burning oneself. You can be grateful for your feelings of guilt, just as you are grateful that you feel a burning sensation when you touch something hot. The message from our inner self to our conscious self is clearly "Ouch! Stop that!" and then, once we've stopped doing whatever is burning us, the cry becomes "Make it better!"

Consider a person working in a factory and inadvertently burning himself on some piece of machinery. What is the immediate instinctual response? To pull away (stop doing that thing which causes the burning.) What is the next likely thing that the worker will do? Find some water or ice to cool the burn (i.e., make it better: In the emotional realm, this stage would involve making amends when possible.) Now, after having had this experience, how likely do you think it is that the worker will reach out and touch that machinery again in the future?

This analogy illustrates the healthy function of guilt in our lives. Unfortunately, it can be a little more complicated in the emotional realm than in the physical. This is because when we are physically wounded, our instinctual responses do much of the work for us. In contrast, when we feel the emotional pangs of guilt, we have to interpret those feelings and consciously decide on a course of action.

Now let me twist the analogy to show you what it would look like if someone was engaging in shame instead of healthy, transitory guilt. Consider how absurd it would be for the injured worker to refuse to douse his burn with water, claiming he deserved the pain because he had touched the burning metal. What if he refused medical attention in favor of isolating himself in a room where he continually replayed the event in his mind, telling himself how stupid, inept, careless, and burned he was? He could even sink to telling himself that there was something inherently wrong with him that made him different from other people and more prone to burn himself. With attitudes like this about himself, he would probably end up burning himself again. Then he might even come

33

to believe that he was incapable of walking through a factory without burning himself.

Of course it is easy to see how absurd, unhealthy, and unhelpful it would be for the factory worker to abuse himself in this way. Now replace the hot machinery with a mistake or a sin that you have committed. Replace the factory with the context in which it happened, such as a relationship, a job interview, a family gathering, a date, a talk with your daughter/son, etc. Ask yourself, how do you treat yourself when you mess up? What about when you *really* mess up? Is it more like the first example or the second example of the worker?

Guilt has its purpose, but don't let it wear out its welcome and turn into shame. It should not lead to a lengthy period of self-abasement and self-criticism. Shame is a voice that wants to punish you and never let you out of its grip. Shaming thoughts become self-fulfilling prophecies. If all day long you tell yourself that you are bad, then you are going to start living up to that claim more and more all the time. And what do bad people do? They do bad things.

The hardest part of my job is to convince people that anger directed at themselves is destructive and they need to stop hurting themselves. The more that my clients cling to their feelings of shame, the longer they take to get well. The guilt just eats away at them, until, sooner or later, they act out on their shame and hurt someone again when they are angry.

It is ironic that many people start abusing themselves with these shame-based thoughts because they *are* so sorry for what they have done. They wish they had never made that mistake, and hope fervently that they will never err in that way again. It is like whipping themselves to prove their contrition to God or themselves, and perhaps make some sort of atonement. However **the end result of engaging in this constant negative self-talk is that they do more of the behavior that they despise.**

In order to be well and whole, people must not only release their anger about all the times they have been hurt, they must also forgive themselves for hurting others. This forgiveness of ourselves is much harder for two reasons. First, you have to face what you have done wrong. Second, you have to avoid the impulse to punish yourself, and instead receive forgiveness. If you struggle in this area, I encourage you to read the section of this book called "What to Do When You've Really Messed Up."

My most successful clients accept forgiveness, then work very hard at loving others. They do lots of Anger Work, but they do not act-out their anger on themselves or on others.

Key #2: No Taking Out Your Anger On Others

The second key to doing successful Anger Work is never to focus the expression of your anger directly on another person while in his or her presence. Screaming at people is not Anger Work if those people are there to hear you. It might feel great for the moment, and release those intense feelings of rage, but it does not have the same benefits as real Anger Work.

One problem that comes with aiming your anger at others, even when you feel justified, is that it can feed into a cycle of abuse, which is hard to break out of. By this I mean that your abuse of another can motivate that person to treat you abusively, which in turn causes you to feel angry and want to get back at him or her and so the cycle continues. When marital or family feuds occur, both sides usually have genuine grievances and feel justified in taking vengeance. But their vengeance just continues the cycle of abuse.

In extreme forms, this abuse can go on for many generations. Classic examples of this are Romeo and Juliet, gang violence, and the conflicts occurring in many countries around the world today. Closer to home is the reality that we have to be careful not to let the same thing happen on a smaller scale within our own families. Husband and wife or parent and child can get so deeply entrenched in a battle of wills that they don't know how to break out of it. They keep hurting each other in spite of their love for one another.

Each time you express your anger in an abusive way, you make it that much easier for yourself to be abusive again in the future. You build up a tolerance for violence and discord. It feels natural and normal to you. Especially if you surround yourself with other abusive people. It can get to the point where you have no accurate picture of how abusive you have become.

When I was young, I knew a couple who were friends of our family. My dad grew up with Chris in a small town in Iowa. Chris's mother had a very harsh temper, and as he grew up, Chris took on this mean spirit. He got married to Mary in his early twenties. She had the same hot temper that he did, maybe even a little worse. Evidently they started out just having little squabbles, but the longer they were married, the worse their fights got.

They had four kids, none of whom were spared from these rages. As the years went by, the abuse escalated. Finally one day when Chris was at work, Mary broke the arm of one of their children in a fit of rage. She didn't realize how out of control that she'd gotten with her anger; I'm not sure she ever realized how inappropriate her behavior was. She was very sorry about the broken arm, but they did not seek medical attention for their son Teddy because no one knew about the incident except Mary, Chris, and poor Teddy, and they wanted to keep it that way. The shame was so intense that they even denied their child the medical treatment he needed just so that they could cover up for themselves. Many years later, Chris told my dad the story, and that is how I learned what happened.

How did it get that bad? You've probably heard the analogy of the frog and the pot of boiling water. If you put a frog in a pot of hot water, it will jump out immediately and save itself. But if you put a frog in a pot of cool water and heat it very gradually, the frog gets used to the temperature little by little and doesn't detect the danger. It will sit there and boil to death. That is essentially what happened to Chris and his wife. The conflict and violence in their home escalated gradually until Teddy really got hurt. They were at the boiling point and never even saw it coming.

Sometimes finding the self-control to follow this guideline of not acting out your anger at others can be very difficult. If you are like most people, when someone hurts you, you want to hurt them back. Perhaps you have greatly injured another person by lashing back at him or her in anger. At the time of your angry outburst, you probably felt justified in your reaction. You might say, "My son was caught smoking pot at school when I told him that I wish he'd never been born." Or maybe you would say, "My friend gossiped about a very private matter. She deserved what I said to her." Or I've heard men tell me, "My wife was screaming and I warned her that she'd better shut up before I slapped her."

We may rationalize "an eye for an eye and a tooth for a tooth." Or as children regularly say, "She hit me first!" So what is wrong with hurting another person if that person hurt you first? Much. When you choose to hurt another person, you have to live with the consequences of your behavior, not just the *external* consequences to your relationship with that person, but the ***internal*** consequences of living with what you've done.

This brings us to the most crucial reason not to act-out your anger on others. Namely, that each time you hurt another person you create one more thing that you have to forgive yourself for. And forgiving oneself is the most daunting obstacle that exists on the path to healing. The reason it's so difficult is that when you hurt another in anger, no matter how justified you may feel at the time, later shame will creep in. Shame is like a little voice that follows you around and whispers in your ear, telling you that you don't deserve a good life. If you're not very careful, shame will sabotage your healing and keep you from getting well.

Over years of working with a variety of people, I have seen people try very hard to justify their abusive behavior. This kind of rationalization is a poor substitute for self-forgiveness. It is based on self-deception rather than acceptance and repentance. Regardless of how hard you try to rationalize your guilt away, you carry with you the knowledge of what you have done. It is like a big pimple on your face: you have to spend a great deal of time and effort constantly covering it up so that it isn't the first thing you see when you look in the mirror. The worse your offense, the larger the blemish is.

You may rationalize the wrong that you've done and manage to relegate it to the back of your mind, but you will not be happy. You cannot be truly happy unless you can be honest with yourself. People who have been very abusive to others have trouble doing this because when they start looking inside, they generally encounter self-hatred and shy away.

If you will not grapple with the shame and allow yourself to feel the pain and anger (which are the psyche's natural responses to your own failure), then you cannot feel happy either, at least not naturally. This is because when we repress our unwanted emotions, the desirable ones get shoved away too. We cannot be selective. That's why so many people turn to drugs to suppress their unwanted feelings and get that artificial "high" that simulates happiness. But getting "high" is a fleeting and shallow substitute for genuine peace and happiness.

The more things you do to harm others, the more shame you have to heal from. It is true that victims sometimes feel shame over the degrading abuse that they have experienced; however, this is much more easily overcome in therapy than the shame you feel over times that you yourself were abusive to others. As surprising as it is, time and time again I have found it to be true that the most important factor in a victim's recovery from abuse is not what happened to him or her, but rather what s/he did in response to what happened.

If you choose to hurt others in response to your own pain, then you will be in therapy much longer. People who hurt others extremely severely, such as raping someone or committing murder, rarely ever become fully functioning because of the tremendous amount of courage and strength that it requires to sort through those memories and receive forgiveness.

One man I worked with had been sexually abused as a child by his father. He felt powerless to do anything back to his dad, so he channeled his anger toward someone weaker than himself. He sexually abused his younger brother for several years while they were growing up.

At the time of the abuse, he tried hard not to think about what damage his behavior might be inflicting and rationalized that everyone has sexual needs. He told himself, "If I lived through it, so can he. After all, he deserves it, the little brat." We all know that this type of abuse can be incredibly damaging to the victim, but what we often fail to see is that it can be <u>even more</u> damaging to the abuser. If you do not believe this, just imagine how you would feel looking in your mirror knowing that you had been the perpetrator of such a crime.

When this client reached adulthood, he entered therapy and started working through the issues surrounding his own abuse. It was during this process that he realized how serious his crime against his brother was. The intensity of his shame was overwhelming. He tried hard to apologize for his abusive behavior, but to little avail. His brother, who is now a drug addict, does not want to talk about the abuse. This man has spent many years in torment over his choice. He continues to work at forgiving himself, but it is very hard, and he still suffers from serious bouts with depression.

Though the consequences are not obvious in less extreme cases, they are still there; this principle holds true regardless of the severity of the offense. **When you say mean things or act abusively toward others, you extend the time that it will take for you to become whole, and you make your own recovery more difficult.** You must try to avoid being unkind to people even in small ways, not only for their sakes, but for your own as well.

One of my professional and personal interests has been to interview people who have been extremely abusive and see how they feel about their abusive behavior. When I ask the questions in a non-shaming way, people usually confess to their horrible guilt and shame. They do not let others see this because they feel so bad already that they don't want others to hurt them any further. It is like a child who won't let you take out her splinter for fear that it will make it hurt more than it already does.

One of my clients, Michael, was a good example of this. He had cheated on his wife several times and hated himself for his behavior. But because his guilt was so painful, he tried to hide that tender spot from everyone. He portrayed anger to those he loved in order to shield his wounds of shame. Many people use this same coping mechanism.

If we come to understand this behavior pattern, their actions will make a lot more sense to us. Some people think that if they act like a grizzly bear on the outside, they can avoid getting hurt because no one will come close enough to hurt them. Well, they're right about one thing; no one can come close. The problem is that this isolation brings its own kind of pain. In addition, by being harsh and abusive with others, they only add to that mound of shame that they are trying to hide. It makes for a miserable existence. In working so hard to make sure that no one else hurts them, they usually end by hurting themselves at least as badly.

In contrast to this reality, most television shows, movies, and novels make it seem as if abusers have no conscience. The classic villain is a person who can carry out all sorts of dastardly deeds without a twinge of conscience. This antagonist is wicked to the bone and can grin with genuine (albeit perverse) pleasure as he causes others to suffer.

Many of us come to believe that this is a realistic picture of our own abusers, and that this is how we would feel if we ever decided to go down that same path. Well, before you feel too tempted and start thinking "if you can't beat 'em, join 'em," let me assure you that this is not the case. It is a very inaccurate portrayal of how life really is.

In reality, abusers hate themselves and their lives, even if they don't show it to the outside world. The only exception to this is a sociopath, and sociopaths are very rare. So rare, in fact that chances are you've never known one. So we must not think that all the bad people in our lives are sociopaths. Your abusers feel shame and suffer when they hurt you. Sometimes remembering this fact makes it easier to hold back from lashing out. Rest assured that they will reap what they have sown. You don't have to dirty your own hands by trying to get involved in the process.

If you are still not convinced that abusive behavior produces a miserable life, try to think of five people whom you have known personally or known about who were mean and cruel to others during their lives. Look and see how their lives turned out. Sometimes you will have to wait until they are older to see the results. Who still loves them? How is their quality of life?

Just maybe, one of them will tell you how he or she spent much of his or her life in self-hatred. They guard this secret very well because they are in such torment that they do not want to let others have a chance to inflict further wounds. Their lives end up so horribly because they hate themselves.

Abusive people can choose to change, but that involves taking a long, hard, honest look at themselves, facing what they've done, and then working through the shame, pain, sorrow, and anger. Because this is so difficult, most chronically abusive people choose to keep acting-out on others and avoid self-reflection.

You see, someone who has been abused but chose not to become an abuser can find the courage, given a supportive environment, to face the memories of their abuse and do Anger Work about them. People who responded to their abuse by coming abusers can do this as well about their own abuse, but that alone won't be enough to make them whole. They will also need to work through the memories of times when they abused others.

This is where many people fail or get stuck. They refuse to work through these memories either because they cannot bear their own feelings of shame, or because they are afraid of losing the approval of their therapist or others. So they give up on themselves and give up trying to work through their feelings. Instead they find some addiction, or fall into depression or psychosomatic illness to avoid their feelings. It is not that they are incapable of healing, but that they will not face up and then forgive themselves for their crimes. This lack of forgiveness causes a perpetuation of the cycle of abuse.

I see this situation sometimes in my practice. A client will come in for help because something in his or her life is troublesome. Perhaps a bad marriage, headaches, or depression is the presenting problem. We start working on the presenting problem, and I do the usual exploration of the past. When an event that the client feels shame about is identified or starting to be unearthed, some people will choose to quit therapy and live with the symptoms rather than face their own feelings of shame.

I don't ever feel angry at my clients when this happens. I feel sad, because I know that the shame can be healed if the person is brave and willing. I know that by refusing to look at their pain, their problems will only get worse and affect the lives of those around them as well.

This is a very important concept to grasp. Remember, the biggest stumbling block on the road to healing is not what was done to you by others, but what you did to others. The more shame-inducing memories you create for yourself, the more potholes and falling rock you'll find on your road to recovery. **In terms of recovery outlook, how *abused* you are doesn't matter as much as how *abusive* you are.** This is why it is an essential key to a successful Anger Work to stop acting-out your anger on others.

Those who keep acting-out their anger are very hard for me to help as a therapist. On the flip side, when clients learn to release their anger in appropriate ways and are nice to others, I find that they do incredibly well.

One man with whom I worked had a very gentle soul and tried hard never to hurt anyone, though he had sustained some severe childhood abuse and was in an abusive marriage. First he had to learn to get angry about his abuse instead of being depressed. But once he did that, he quickly learned to release the anger through appropriate Anger Work. He also learned to be more firm in setting boundaries with others while remaining kind. As a result he got well faster than he, I, or any of his friends expected.

Remember, Anger Work is an alternative to being abusive or depressed when you are struggling with anger, loss, failure, or victimization. Anger Work only serves to heal your pain permanently if it is not the cause of personal guilt later. When directing anger at another, there is always the possibility of hurting the other person with your angry response and feeling guilty later. This usually leads to a feeling of being ashamed, and that shame can keep you from being healed. I emphasize that the habit of taking out your anger through actions and unkind words expressed directly at people is often what keeps a person from getting emotionally well.

When you do your Anger Work, your anger must always be expressed in ways in which no one gets hurts. If you hit a punching bag instead of the teacher who failed you in a course, there is no cause to worry about repercussions later. Guilt will not be a worry, since you did not hurt anyone. Yet you will still experience the catharsis of expressing the anger, and be completely healed.

If you are someone who has been abusive in the past and now you want to change and be healed, first start replacing your angry, hurtful responses to others with real Anger Work. Then let the section of this book called "What to Do When You Mess Up" help guide you into self-forgiveness.

A Special Note about Animals

As I have pointed out, anger must not be directed at others; this includes animals. Any sensate creature that can experience pain as a result of your wrath must be avoided when you are expressing your anger. Animals have feelings too, and cruelly hurting or frightening them will not be good for you. If you choose to do your Anger Work by directing your anger at a particular object, you need to make sure that it is an inanimate object, not an animal or person.

I am a real animal lover. As such, it comes as a confession to admit that as a growing boy in Iowa I hunted a great deal. In order to do this, I had to suppress my love of animals whenever I went hunting. After having lived in California for a few years, I returned home to Iowa for the holidays. Once again, I went hunting and shot and killed four rabbits. I did not intend to eat the animals, I just wanted to experience the "joy" of hunting. Prior to hunting this time, I had been in therapy for a couple of years and was more in touch with my feelings. To my surprise, I felt no joy, only sadness and remorse. Things had changed for me. I grieved for those little bunnies, and needless to say, I have never been hunting since.

When working with children, I check to see how my young clients are treating their pets. If they are being cruel, this impedes their healing. I love animals so much that I have the children bring their animals to therapy. I have had snakes, dogs, cats, rabbits, pigs, etc., come to visit. This helps youngsters bond with me and we have a great time. If you have a child who is cruel to animals, I recommend that you seek help. Remember that he or she is not only hurting the animals, but him or herself as well.

If you have pets, treat them kindly and do not do your Anger Work on them. If you really feel a need to do Anger Work on animals, choose stuffed animals. My adult clients as well as children have destroyed many of my stuffed animals as they pretend that the animals are the abusers who hurt them. But real animals have feelings, and cruelly hurting animals will cause you to feel guilt and shame, which will not be good for you. It will only impede your recovery and give you that much more to recover from.

You are probably starting to see the connection between abusing yourself and abusing others. The more you abuse yourself with shame, the more you will fall into negative self-fulfilling prophecies. This leads right into making more mistakes and hurting more people. The more habitually you abuse others, the more your feelings of guilt (I <u>did</u> something bad) will turn into shame (I <u>am</u> bad) and the whole thing becomes circular.

Even when someone is abusive to you, do not sink to the same level. Go ahead and set up boundaries, speak out about injustices, call the police, or defend yourself physically if necessary, but never take an eye for eye, or in your wrath, rationalize cruel behavior. Later, when you calm down, you will have to look yourself in the mirror. Try to make it easy for yourself to like what you see.

A Special Note on Substance Abuse

Substance Abuse is a topic that deserves special note. This is partly because it is such a widespread problem, and partly because it provides such a perfect example of how circular self-abuse and abuse of others can be. Drug and alcohol abuse illustrate for us how self-abuse is really abusive to others, and how abusing others really ends up being self-abusive as well.

When I was doing my internship at the Veterans Hospital in Los Angeles, I attended a lecture by four psychologists and psychiatrists who had each had about twenty-five years of experience working with clients recovering from severe alcohol and drug abuse. The doctors all admitted that the best results that they had ever seen in their work with these recovering addicts was to lessen their symptoms to a point of low level depression.

The addicts would stop using their drug of choice and get involved in intensive group and individual therapy. They would re-enter the home and workplace, but the best that they could expect was to live with depression the rest of their lives. Hearing that deeply troubled me. I couldn't understand why their clients wouldn't get completely well.

After years of pondering this, asking myself why, and after personal experience working with recovering substance abusers, I decided what I think it is. I believe the main (though not the only) reason that severe addicts have such a hard time rising above their depression is due to the intense shame that results from all the regrettable things that they have done while "under the influence."

When people use drugs, including alcohol, they lose impulse control. In other words, their normal constraints are gone and they cannot control their behavior as well as they usually would. As a result, severe substance abusers have almost always committed some if not numerous acts of abuse against others. I find that people who commit serious crimes or cheat on their spouses are almost always drinking or under the influence of some substance at the time. I had worked with one man only a couple of times when he told me that he had sexually molested his cousin's daughter while the mom was away for a few hours. He said it was because his behavior just felt natural after he took some "crack."

Kurt Cobain was a famous rock star who committed suicide. He was a heroin addict, and he confessed in his notes that he was losing control of his impulse to hurt his daughter when she cried, so he killed himself. He clearly loved his daughter, but he needed to love himself enough to seek help and receive forgiveness.

When I work with recovering drug addicts, my first and foremost efforts are to listen to their stories of how they have hurt those that they've loved. When they stop using drugs, they are confronted with their past errors and sins. They must come to terms with all the times that they have hurt people in their lives, and this is extremely difficult. I listen and accept them completely.

It's not that the world judges them so harshly, but they judge themselves mercilessly.

Over the course of time, I have worked with many cases in which the addict is a parent and spouse. Once he or she stops using and seeks help, the spouse and children rejoice. This love is what helps the recovering addict to heal, if he or she will receive it. I remind my patients, that self-criticism only puts them back into the downward spiral and leads to repeated harmful behavior. I help them realize that seeking treatment, forgiving themselves, and healing from their own pain are the most loving things they can do for their spouse and children. If the patient wants to be a good parent and spouse, then he must learn to forgive himself.

As you may have already guessed, I encourage people to stay away from drugs and alcohol because of this impulsive-control problem. When people cannot control themselves, they are more likely to hurt others. When the drug wears off, they have to face themselves in the mirror. The shame can be overwhelming. Reflect on your life and think about some time when you hurt someone in anger. I'm sure you will agree that the memories are hard to heal.

When you make the choice to do drugs, you are making the choice to turn over control of your impulses. Sometimes the only power you have over your own actions is the power to choose not to abuse the substance in the first place.

If you do Anger Work to rid yourself of stress and bottled-up feelings, then you will be free to experience the genuine happiness and enjoyment that life has to offer. You will not need to turn to drugs to make yourself feel good. With the tools of Anger Work, you can face whatever is bothering you instead of trying to escape it. That way you can actually work through your pain or anger instead of letting it hang onto you for years, leading you into unhealthy behavior. This approach requires more effort in the short run, but in the long run can mean the difference between loving life and hating it.

Anger Work Methods

When thinking of ways to express their anger, most people want to do something vengeful towards the object of their fury. But there are many other options. In this chapter, I would like to describe some of the numerous forms that Anger Work can take. If you have already started your personal recovery, I trust that you will find in this section some tangible methods for taking ownership of your healing process. You can use these ideas on your own or in a therapy session. Applying these strategies will speed up your recovery and help you learn to live life to the fullest limits of human potential.

Anger Work through Exercise

My favorite form of Anger Work is exercise. As part of my fitness regimen, I do an hour or two of some form of exercise every day, and I have for the last twenty years. At this point in my life, I have learned to work through my issues pretty quickly as they arise, so most days I don't have anything that I need to do Anger Work about. But if anything should arise, such as the recent death of my brother-in-law, this gives me an avenue for regularly dealing with my feelings and not letting them fester. I am assured that twenty-four hours will not pass before I can deal with my anger. I find that my clients who work out regularly do better than those who do not.

The types of exercise routines are too numerous to mention in this book. If you've ever watched the Olympics, you know how many different events there are. Your exercise of choice could range from an intense form of professional athletic training to a nice walk in the park for half an hour each day. You can get some information about working out from books, magazines, professional trainers, or people you know who work out regularly. **Any form of exercise can be used as an effective way to express anger.**

If you have not been exercising regularly, you must start slowly. You will want to talk to your medical doctor and possibly find a personal trainer to help you get started. If you work your way up gradually, you will be able to stick with it. The great thing about using exercise to do your Anger Work is that there are so many positive side effects, such as stress reduction, mood regulation, and physical fitness.

Intensity is not as important as commitment and regularity. Anger Work takes time. If you lost your child in an accident with a drunk driver, you may need to go for hundreds, if not thousands of angry walks or swims to get over this loss. Just stick with it and eventually you will be healed completely.

I love exercise, but **exercise alone is not enough to heal us from our emotional wounds.** After spending over twenty years going to gyms, I know that many people who exercise are unhappy and/or depressed. You must do some form of Anger Work while exercising. **What is important is that you feel the anger.** Anger is an empowering emotion that will help yank you out of depression and the victim mentality.

For example, you can practice boxing a punching bag as you feel anger and think about how your boss just fired you for some unjustified reason. Or you may be with some friends at a bowling alley, throwing the balls at your ex-wife who cheated on you. You may be out rowing in a river, pretending to hit your father's hand with a paddle for slapping you across the face when you were eleven years old.

Years ago in my practice, I helped a wonderful middle-aged woman who lived with her mother. This client had a heart of gold, but she had been mentally delayed since birth. She came to therapy because of some anxiety that she was having at her work and at home.

Gradually I discovered that her mother was controlling and bossy. My client had never expressed her anger. So I encouraged her to start walking daily and to think about her mother's bossiness while she was walking. She was to pretend to step on her mother as she walked. This worked wonders. My client's anxiety subsided; she was able to get her anger out by walking. She felt better and was able to stand up to her mother's demands. Her Anger Work was so simple and effective that I have never forgotten her.

You don't always have to do something back to the other person in your mind. Sometimes just thinking about some injustice is enough to release the anger. For example, you may enjoy running. You could run and also think about how your eight-year-old peers used to tease you about your protruding ears. By doing this you release your anger in the form of energy that propels you to run.

If it bothers you to focus your Anger Work on a specific person, you can focus on being angry that people can be so cruel, and imagine that you are taking out your anger on the evil that exists in the world. This is too abstract for most people, which is why most of the examples that I am listing focus on the abuser. However, for some people, having an abstract object for their Anger Works better than anything else.

The benefits of Exercise Anger Work are manifested in my private practice. As of this date, I have never had to hospitalize any of my clients. When someone who is suicidal pages me, first I listen to them on the phone. Then I ask them to go walk for half an hour or more. I make them promise that if they are still suicidal when they finish their walk, they will give me a call back. So far I have never received a second phone call, and no one has committed suicide. When I see these clients at the next meeting, they always tell me that they felt much better after the walk, and did not need to talk to me again until our next meeting.

Doing exercise is a great idea for when you are really upset. For example, let's say that your husband had gotten a tip from a friend and invested a large sum of money in the stock market. Some months later he came home and reported that he had lost it all. You got upset because the two of you had been saving for a down payment on a house. Instead of blasting him, why not walk or ride your bike, calm down, and then talk to him?

When I see married couples together in therapy, I never allow them to shout or say destructive things to each other. This is hurtful and unproductive. If you know that the topic you need to discuss with a loved one is going to create upset feelings for either of you, I suggest you take a walk together and talk about the subject while you are walking. This will give you an avenue to release anger or tension by walking instead of directing it at the other person. Keep walking until you both calm down.

I always walk during lunchtime. Sometimes I walk to get my food, or I eat in my office first and then walk. Other times I walk and eat at the same time. Whenever I get a break, I go for a walk. I just quickly change shoes and go. Years ago when I used to work in a medical office suite, the nurses would tease me because I would come back from a long lunch walk quite sweaty on hot days. I still come back sweaty sometimes, but I don't see this as a problem. The air conditioner always cools me down and none of my clients complain about my perspiration. They see that I am simply (if you'll pardon the pun) "walking my talk."

Walking is almost always safe, and it's a wonderful way to exercise and do Anger Work when needed. All my friends who are in their eighties and still healthy are walkers. In a few instances, I have known people who could not walk because of intense pain or disability. In those cases I recommend swimming or some upper body exercise.

If you really get into doing your Anger Work through exercise, you may end up like a hiking friend of mine, who was in her late seventies and went on a ten-day backpack with me. We averaged ten miles a day and her pack weighed around forty pounds when we started. We climbed all the way up to about twelve thousand feet! Some of you may think that she just had good genes, but I know a lot of people in their seventies and eighties who are healthy and full of energy. They are all walkers. The year I ran in a marathon, a ninety-two-year old man also ran and finished the race. Please don't let age keep you from the benefits of Anger Work through exercise.

As I discussed earlier, some of my insight into the effectiveness of Anger Work has come from working with children in my clinical practice. In therapy, if a child is given a safe and unstructured environment, he or she will typically go to my toy chest and find great pleasure in destroying my toys. I resupply my toy box by getting used and discarded toys from other children. Sometimes children like to hit things; other times they prefer to shoot at them with my toy guns. Some adults, I've found, like to do the same thing. In my toy chest, I keep several different types of plastic bats and toy guns, which both children and adults can use when doing Anger Work on the toys.

Anger Work through Hitting Things

Hitting things is one of the most popular ways people do Anger Work. You can take hold of a bat and start pounding away on a bed, couch, toy, or an object that represents the person with whom you are angry. Some people prefer to use their hands instead of a bat. Either way works just as well, as long as you are not hurting yourself.

Be careful not to use an object that either of you or someone else will miss if it is destroyed. If it is precious to someone else, it would throw you back into that guilt/shame cycle again if you destroy it. If it is precious to you, the loss will detract from the benefits of the Anger Work.

The point of this Anger Work is not just to pound on something. You need to attempt to focus on your feelings about some issue or event in your life that still causes you to feel angry, hurt, or sad. It is not necessary to focus on a specific event; you may simply allow your feelings to flow into your actions, and start hitting.

Anger Work through Shooting and Throwing Things

Just as hitting things is a natural means to work out our anger, so is aiming projectiles at an object. Shooting or throwing things can be a very effective Anger Work method. This may include rock throwing, dart throwing, shooting toy guns, or going to a real shooting range.

Some people enjoy and greatly benefit from throwing rocks as a form of anger therapy. This can be done while out in nature or in the city, by skipping rocks into a body of water, or using a nearby rock pile. One of my clients was a boy who loved to throw rocks at a rock mound near my work place. He and I would both throw rocks; he would always feel better afterward. Since then, I have done therapy with other boys, girls, and several adults who enjoy utilizing this technique.

For those of you who want a specific object to focus your Anger Work on, I have a couple of suggestions. First, you can try using a photo or a drawing of your abuser and throw darts or shoot toy guns at it. A second option is to pretend that some toy is a "bad guy" and shoot it with a toy gun. I keep a variety of toy guns at my office. As you may guess, they are very popular with the kids and even with some of my adult clients.

If you are an adult who needs a more intense form of Anger Work, you may want to try going to a shooting range where they rent both guns and ammo. Shooting a real gun can be scary and emotionally traumatizing, so I do not recommend this form of Anger Work for everyone. Going with a friend is recommended if you decide to do it.

At the shooting range, they instruct you in how to shoot the gun, and then let you use it on your own. They have targets with circular rings like a classic bull's-eye, or life-sized silhouettes of a man or woman. You could pretend that it is the man who raped you, or you may prefer to imagine it as a potential attacker, and how you would deal with that now that you are empowered and no longer a victim.

Anger Work through Scream Release

Another popular way to do Anger Work is through scream release work. There are two ways to go about this. The first technique is rather simple: just let out a yell. In my own therapy, when I was finally able to scream, I was sure that the world was going to come to an end. I still remember screaming as I was driving in my car. I was so surprised to find that I was fine and felt much better. I had had several years of therapy and lots of Anger Work prior to coming to this point, so you may not get the same intense release of emotion at first. But letting go of your deep inner anger can be very satisfying. Please be a little careful or you may lose your voice as I did the first time I tried screaming.

The second scream technique is to pretend that you are yelling at the person who has hurt you. Gestalt therapy has used this therapeutic technique for years. A Gestalt therapist puts an empty chair in front of his or her patient and has the patient "talk to" the abuser. You may do this or just pretend that the person can hear you. Go ahead and tell him/her what you think about what he/she did. Tell the person why you are upset and how he or she has hurt you.

Many people are, of course, afraid that other people may hear them and wonder what they will think. This is a valid concern for which I have found several remedies. First, you can find a pillow or two, and scream into them. Add on more if you think that others can hear you. The noise may sound a little loud to you, but you can tape record or ask a close friend to listen to the sound to ensure that it's not loud enough for anyone to hear you.

Secondly, you can scream while you are driving alone in your car, if you have one. While driving at a normal speed with the windows up, no one will hear you. However, you must also concentrate on driving to ensure that you don't lose control.

Thirdly, you could go to a musical concert or sporting event where screaming is part of the ambiance and you have freedom to yell. Everyone else will think you're just a devoted fan!

A fourth way that I have found effective is to go somewhere in the wilderness where you are alone and let your angry voice ring through the hills. I am an outdoor person, and once in a while, I will go backpacking during the winter in the mountains where no one is around. At night I am always totally alone except for the few animals that inhabit the wild. This provides the perfect opportunity for scream release Anger Work, if I need it. Before venturing out on your own expedition in the wild, please get training and experience with others.

One of my clients walks and screams along the beach when there is no one around and when the waves are crashing, drowning out the sound of her voice. She "talks to" the abuser in a loud voice, telling him how furious she is at him.

Screaming underwater is another great way to express anger in solitude. No one will hear you. As you can see, there are many creative and effective ways to do scream release Anger Work. If you come up with any more ways of screaming without being heard by other, please let me know.

Anger Work When You're Not Alone

Many times people ask me how they can express their anger when overt methods would not be appropriate. This might be in a classroom or workplace, or in a car with your spouse when you are angry with him or her. You do not have the level of privacy that you need to do the typical forms of Anger Work. You do not want to draw attention to yourself, or frighten the person you are with, but you know that you need to get those feelings out because you can feel the pressure rising. You don't want to blow-up at the person, or get another one of those wretched tension headaches. So, what can you do? In addition to setting good boundaries and being as assertive as you can without becoming aggressive, I have some Anger Work suggestions for you.

You might want to use the hand-squeezing technique. You may let your anger out by simply rolling one or both hands up into a fist and squeezing. If you hide your hands, no one will notice. You could also press down on the floor with your feet or tighten the muscles in some other part of the body. These are forms of isometric exercise that you can do when you are with people.

If the situation is especially aggravating, you are going to need to address it again during your private Anger Work time; however these techniques should help you make it through the conversation or situation, and you can deal with the rest later.

Many people clench their jaws or contract the muscles in their neck and shoulders in an unconscious reaction to stress. This frequently leads to headaches, sore muscles, and conditions such as T.M.J. Instead of *reacting* to stress in these harmful ways, why not proactively **respond** to it. Teach your mind and body to work together to bring about greater health for yourself as a whole being.

If you decide that you like these isometric techniques enough, you can incorporate them into your regular Anger Work as well. The hand-squeezing exercise may be done while walking. As a variation, you can use a tennis ball for squeezing or make a ball out of wax.

Anger Work on the Road

For my readers who spend a lot of time in their vehicle every day, I have a couple of suggestions. First, while you are driving, you can squeeze the steering wheel and let your anger out. Or you can pound away on the seat or door next to you, or the dash board. Hitting the windshield is not recommended for obvious safety reasons.

Don't forget the yelling techniques as well; they will probably be the most useful to you in a driving situation. People rarely take the time to really look at the other people driving by, and if someone does see you yelling, you will probably never see them again. If you like, you can use a trick that a friend taught me. She is a singer and loves to sing at the top of her lungs in her car. She doesn't care if anyone sees her singing, but she feels shy about being seen screaming. So, when she is really mad about something, she either makes up a sarcastic song and belts it out to express her anger, or she simply taps her fingers on the steering wheel to make it look like she is keeping time with the beat on the radio while she yells with gusto!

Sooner or later, anyone who drives will encounter a rude driver, but those rude drivers can actually be helpful to you. First, remember not to act-out your anger by being rude back to them. I usually wave and smile when someone cuts me off in traffic, but as soon as they are out of my sight, I say what I think about their driving. This may seem insincere at first, but in truth I do wish the person well. I am simply angry at them at that moment, but that is something I can deal with on my own.

For many people, anger is easily triggered while driving, including my clients who have a difficult time getting angry elsewhere. Carol was a client whom I worked with who could never bring herself to do Anger Work on a planned basis; however, she felt very angry whenever someone cut her off on the freeway. I encouraged her to go ahead and use these aggravating situations to work on her anger. Since she lived in Los Angeles and commuted to and from work five days a week, she had lots of opportunities to express her anger. As a result of this Anger Work, the stomach pains that she had been experiencing from repressed feelings gradually went away.

I encourage you to release the anger that you feel while driving. You may find as Carol did, that it helps you to release other repressed feelings, unrelated to the moment. You can use the anger you feel at everyday experiences to help you heal. Perhaps you ride the bus to work every day and half the time the bus is late. You could use this time to let your anger out. Hand-squeezing, doing isometric tightening and loosening of other muscles, writing or drawing about your anger, and muttering under your breath are great outlets. Be creative and think of your own methods. Just remember to focus on expressing your anger while you're doing it.

You may have been severely abused by someone while growing up, but feel no anger, or have little or no memory of the events. Your local bus driver may give you lots of opportunities to heal from your past abuse, as his habit of being late produces anger and the anger triggers memories.

Remember, the important thing is to spend time regularly with your anger and let it out. If you never direct it at anyone, then you will never have to worry about hurting someone else. But take equal care not to undermine your own physical health. Repressed emotions create physical tension and emotional stress. Many medical conditions are partially, if not completely, stress-induced. Holding on to your anger is what may kill you. Doing safe Anger Work will heal.

A few times a week, try to convert the energy generated from how upset you felt when people treated you badly. Take the energy and use it to fuel your own Anger Work. As you release your anger, you will burn off that energy. It will no longer be lingering in your system. You may find that your headaches, stomachaches, and depression periods are reduced or even disappear.

Artistic Anger Work

My doctoral dissertation was based on analyzing literature and other art forms as a mode of emotional expression. I learned that art work can be an excellent means of self-expression. I have found art can be a very helpful tool in therapy as well. However, my research and experience suggest that the usual creating of art for art's sake is not enough to heal you from the effects of an abusive past. This may help enough to keep you from losing your mind, but it will not bring a person to wholeness and peace.

Using art as a form of Anger Work involves more. All of the children and some of my adult clients love to do Art Anger Work. They may create realistic images with their angry feelings, or they may create and then destroy some piece of art. It is best to let your anger flow as you create. One survivor of sexual abuse may create abstract paintings dominated by deep red tones. Another may create a jumble of body parts expressing the confusion and disconnectedness he feels.

One client I had many years ago was angry at a former therapist who used to eat cookies during their sessions and had even fallen asleep on the client on one occasion. To express this anger, she drew a caricature of her former therapist lounging on the couch with cookie crumbs all over her. Her eyes were heavily lidded, and a little balloon above her head read "Want a cookie?" My client drew herself on the other couch as a nondescript naked body with a huge knife sticking out of her guts and blood pooling on the floor below her. She was careful to include the plaque that hung ironically on her former therapist's wall: it read "It's Never Too Late to Have a Happy Childhood." In this one drawing, the client was able to express her desperate need for help and her anger at feeling neglected by the therapist.

Let your creativity go. Who knows, perhaps you will create some items worth selling someday. A couple of professional artists with whom I have worked over the years in my practice have changed their style of artistic expression after getting into Anger Work. They often feel even more connected to their pieces because of the intense level of self-expression.

Some other modes of artistic expression you may want to explore are those of expressive dance, creative movement, and creative visualization. Yours could be a dance that tells a story, like a ballet does. You do not need to have special training to do this. It is your story. As a whole being, body, mind and spirit, you can express your experience with yourself as the only audience.

Creative movement is different from expressive dance. It can be one, simple, repetitive movement or a series of movements that have symbolic meaning to you. For example as a survivor of rape or sexual abuse, you may create a special work-out routine as one of my clients did.

There were three movements to her routine. The first was a straight, strong punch forward at eye level (with this she imagined punching her attacker in the face.) The second movement was a swift, powerful kick upward (with this she imagined she was kicking the attacker in his private parts.) The third movement brought her arm up over her head, then down in front in a swift swinging motion where her clenched fist met her open palm like a hammer. (This last movement symbolized for her the crushing of the attacker's private parts between an anvil and a large, metal hammer.)

She repeated these movements in sequence for fifteen to twenty minutes at a time several times a week, or whenever she felt the victim mentality taking hold of her again. She found it helped her move from a place of fear and overwhelming vulnerability to a place of empowerment and strength.

Creative Visualization is another tool that you can use. You can pretend that you are a lion ripping up the person who hurt you, or you can imagine a cleansing fire burning away all the evil in a person and leaving behind only that which is good and worthy of remaining. Use your imagination and visualize symbolic scenes that will help you heal.

Here's something fun that you can do with creative visualization. Find a metaphor that works for you and visualize yourself rising above your current problems. You can pretend that you are hiking on the path of life and your particular problems are vines trying to grow around your ankles and keep you from climbing to higher ground. Visualize yourself overcoming that challenge by stomping on them, hacking them up, or simply climbing over them—whatever works for you. Feel the thrill of overcoming those obstacles. This is just one example of what you can do. The possibilities are a limitless as your imagination. Picture yourself as strong, capable, whole, and happy. Then keep doing that Anger Work to make that vision come true.

Journaling

Some people find that they do well with daily journaling as a way to ensure that they get their anger out. It is very similar to the scream release technique in which you "tell" the offending person exactly what you think and feel about them or their actions. The only difference is that your words are written instead of spoken. If you like, you can later read your entry aloud with a supportive close friend or therapist. I have a habit of being sure that at least one person knows all the important things that happen in my life.

Anger Work Focusing on an Event Instead of an Abuser

You will benefit most from Anger Work if you find your own type of expression. As you can see, I have described some intense forms of Anger Work. Some people do better when focusing on the abuser's behavior rather than on the person. Instead of thinking about the abuser and doing Anger Work, they think about what happened and feel their rage about the behavior. Several clients whom I have worked with have had situations in which a family member hurt them in the past, but they have a good relationship with that family member now. They still need to heal from what happened,, but they don't want to ruin the good relationship that they now enjoy.

For example, Jennifer was angry at her father for making the family move away from her friends to a new school where Jennifer felt inferior and rejected. For years she had repressed her anger at her father for having moved into a "nicer neighborhood" where Jennifer suffered the ridicule of several of her new classmates. She loved her father and did not want to risk losing her love for him by focusing her anger on him.

Jennifer learned that she could do Anger Work focusing on her dad's choice to move the family, rather than vilifying someone who was otherwise a nice guy and a good father to her. With this new knowledge, she did her Anger Work and improved immensely. Expressing her anger in this way actually helped her relationship with her father, because she was no longer harboring that old resentment, and this greatly pleased her. Your healing will not be impaired or slowed down if you choose to focus on the offending behavior instead of the person. Choose whatever is most comfortable for you.

Personalize Your Anger Work

As you begin to experiment with Anger Work, I strongly emphasize that you must find what works best for *you*. Find one or more methods, and then do them until you feel healed from your emotional wounds. There is no right or wrong, as long as no one is hurt by the Anger Work. What works wonderfully for one person may be ineffective for another. Often I will give my clients some specific assignments to do. Usually they find that carrying out this Anger Work assignment brings them some relief. However, sometimes the individual will need to modify the method to achieve the desired result.

For example, once I suggested to one of my clients that he pound on his bed with his fists while focusing on the exasperating situation that he was facing at work. So, he went home and tried to work out his anger in this manner. This proved ineffectual for him because, as he said, "I just couldn't get into it." Afterward he went to his neighbor's home where there was a punching bag. He took his bat to the punching bag and found that the sound effects of hitting a wooden bat on a seventy-pound solid bag worked much more effectively for him. You may even find that you choose different avenues of expressing your anger depending on what you are mad about.

Getting Ready to Do Anger Work

In preparing to do your Anger Work, I suggest that you select a private location where no one will hear or see what you are doing unless it is someone who you know understands and supports your work. There are two reasons for this. First, you don't need the complications that might arise as a result of people's lack of understanding. Bystanders who are uncomfortable with the Anger Work process may try to sabotage it by making comments or responding in ways that cause you to feel shame. Remember, there is nothing wrong with being angry, only with hurting people. Don't give other people the chance to make you feel shame for doing what you need to do to heal and become whole.

Secondly, you do not wish to traumatize anyone who might be frightened by an unexpected outburst of anger, even if that anger is not directed toward that individual. It is not fair to others for you to completely disrupt their living environment simply because you are angry, no matter how valid your anger may be. Everyone has a right to a safe-feeling home or work environment. When you infringe upon this right of another human being, you create another reason for yourself to feel guilty, and thus you perpetuate the shame cycle. In doing this you have once again associated the expression of your anger with guilt. The goal is to separate the two so that you can learn to stop feeling bad when you feel mad.

Many people have a hard time being angry. They have spent their lives repressing their anger, often because they are taught that anger is wrong. Or they have seen the effects of anger when it is acted-out on people and they know how much damage unharnessed rage can do. So it may take awhile before you get in touch with intense anger.

Your anger may be expressed very subtly for the first year, like a mouse squeak. Later, it may be like a lion's roar. This is actually a very good way to go. By working into it gradually like this, you will build trust in yourself. This trust is very important, especially if you are someone who has a problem with your temper, or who has always kept everything bottled up inside and feel afraid that you might lose control.

By starting slowly, and gradually increasing the intensity of your anger, you will see that it is possible to get very angry without taking it out on anyone. You can actually learn to vent your anger constructively in a way that will make your life better, not worse! Some of my clients have taken years to build up to the full expression of their anger. Healing will take time, probably years. There is no "quick fix." But don't worry, you will begin to see the benefits right away.

In addition to starting slowly, most clients cycle in their Anger Work patterns. They may have a week or a month of intense Anger Work and then slow down for a while. Then something else will trigger their anger and they get back to their intense Anger Work. Be very patient with yourself and don't overdo it. I sometimes tell my clients that healing is like a long journey, not a sprint or a marathon. If you do not pace yourself, then you may be tempted to quit.

An Example of Anger Work Gone Wrong

I once worked with a family in which the man, Fred, had just found out that he didn't get the promotion he had applied for. What's more, his supervisor had criticized his work as sloppy and said that he would never get moved up if he kept working that way. He got home to his wife and daughter and started yelling about what a *#@~! his boss was, and started punching the walls and furniture. While he was enjoying the cathartic experience of releasing his anger, his family was having quite a different experience. This kind of uncontrolled outburst is just that, it IS NOT ANGER WORK.

Fred's five-year-old daughter, who was too young to understand what was happening, was very frightened by the experience. She felt that something terrible had happened to change her daddy, and she was worried about whether he was going to be okay. She was also afraid that in his anger he might "forget" and accidentally hurt her or her mom. Remember, when children get a cut, they are sincerely afraid they might bleed to death. They have not learned a sense of perspective yet, and a parent's rage can be terrifying for them, even if it is not directed at them.

Fred's wife, Cheryl, told me that she too was afraid. She was worried about the effect this display might have on her daughter. She was also afraid that Fred might destroy something of value. When he had finished "venting," her fear quickly turned to anger as she realized that he had indeed left a large dent in one of the kitchen cabinets, and a ceramic collectible lay broken on the floor.

Fred had reason to be mad. It was a good idea for him to express that anger rather than keep it all bottled-up inside, but it was not a good idea to express it in the way that he did, and especially not at the cost of frightening his daughter. He went about it all wrong. It is not okay to roam around the house smashing things that are of value to yourself or others. It was not fair for Cheryl and their daughter to have to live with a damaged kitchen cabinet daily reminding them of this outburst. Nor would it be fair for the family to have to go to expense of replacing it. By breaking the ceramic figurine, he destroyed something of sentimental value to his wife, and in so doing, he hurt her.

Fred came home from work that day needing to vent his anger and then receive the support of his family. Instead, his choices brought him the exact opposite of what he needed. When he was done, he felt worse than he had before. Now he not only felt like a bad employee, but a bad father and husband as well. Cheryl, whom he could normally rely upon for sympathy and encouragement, didn't even want to talk to him. He made a bad day even worse for himself.

The Cost of Doing Anger Work

The benefits of doing Anger Work are beyond measure. Instead of following in the footsteps of dysfunctional family role models, you can find the freedom to break out of those behavior patterns and become the "you" that you have always wanted to be. Instead of sabotaging your own happiness by repressing your anger (which undermines your physical and emotional health via stress-related illness, obsessive-compulsive behavior, and/or depression) or exploding in anger (which fractures relationships in your life, and causes you to be hounded by guilt), now you can be proactive about resolving your own feelings of anger. You can get mad, and get over it, without all the lingering side effects.

As with anything in life that is truly worthwhile, there is a cost. Now that you have your anger work tools, I encourage you to be brave and think about your past, as much of it as you can, and see what you find. Get out your old photo albums, talk to your old friends and family about your life, or go visit some place in your past and see what feelings arise. Getting these old feelings to surface, and then dealing with them via Anger Work is comparable to clearing all the moldy, disgusting leftovers out of your emotional refrigerator. Doing this type of emotional backtracking is a very serious, though fruitful endeavor. The price of your healing is that you will need to invest your time and energy in this project.

Financial success, owning a nice home, having a good reputation in your field of work, and finding your soulmate are all worthy goals. However, it is possible to have all those and still be unhappy because of depression, anxiety, or other symptoms that come from unresolved emotional issues. Your level of emotional health is the filter through which the rest of your life experiences are perceived. I urge you to ask yourself this question: is there anything more worthy of your time and attention than your own emotional well-being?

Take a moment and think of any person who has achieved greatness, not someone who has inherited riches or won the lottery, but someone who has *achieved* his or her goal. How were they able to accomplish so much? Personal commitment, hard work, and perseverance undoubtedly played a great role. Some of you may think that success has more to do with having good luck or good genes. I encourage you to read the biographies of two or three of your favorite successful people.

Read about Mahatma Gandhi, Abraham Lincoln, Oprah Winfrey, Isaac Newton, Michael Jordan, Marie Curie and see what the important factors were in their lives. You will learn that people who are great achievers are very motivated and work hard to achieve their goals. They spend lots of time and energy developing and maintaining their skills. Achievement of any kind takes time and work.

Make it your highest possible goal to heal from the abuses of your past and become fully you (the "you" you were intended to be, not the one you may have become as a result of being battered by life). To accomplish this you will need to do a lot soul searching. Most people avoid their feelings because they lack the tools necessary to process painful and traumatic events. That is why so many people who were abused as children turn to addictive behavior. You are no longer in that predicament. Now you know what you have to do to work out those emotions and heal.

You simply have to be committed to your own health and make it happen. This entails taking time weekly, or better yet daily, to focus on your repressed feelings and heal them with Anger Work. Of course, the more you work one eliminating your emotional baggage, the quicker you will lighten your load. You will reap great rewards if you will spend the time.

For many of you, this will mean a lot of changes in your life. Usually, our lives are replete with responsibilities and activities that leave little or no time for self-reflection and Anger Work. In order to carve the time out of your schedule, you may have to get good at putting together two letters of the alphabet, 'N' and 'O.' One of my greatest struggles as a therapist is to get people to say "no" to activities so they have time for Anger Work. If you are serious about your emotional health, then you need time to work on it. Saying "no" may not make you popular with others, but not saying "no" has consequences too.

Consequences of Not Doing Anger Work

Emotional neglect is similar to physical neglect. If you eat high fat foods, smoke, and do not exercise for most of your life, then you are taking great risks with your physical health. You may deceptively appear to be in good health for a while, but your body systems are slowly deteriorating. Eventually you will probably develop a grave condition such as cancer, stroke, or heart disease.

Likewise with your emotional health; if you repress your anger year after year, you may not feel the pain for a while, but the problems will come. These problems could include: fractured or dysfunctional relationships, depression, obsessive-compulsive behavior, anxiety, psycho-somatic or stress-induced illnesses, phobias, addictions or a general dissatisfaction with life. If you do not make the time to work out your issues, you will become increasingly dysfunctional. You will hurt other people by lashing out or withdrawing, and you will suffer from feelings of shame. Don't let your life go down that road.

As a whole, people like simple solutions to their problems. Many people turn to prescription drugs instead of feeling their feelings and healing themselves with Anger Work. One of the most puzzling things to me is the fact that anxiety is an emotional disorder, which is not genetic, but is clearly brought on by environmental stress. Scientific studies do not emphasize any inherited component with respect to stress. Yet medical doctors prescribe well over one hundred million forms of anti-anxiety drugs a year.

I rarely get a referral for someone who is stressed and is taking some anti-anxiety drug. This is because if the drugs take away their symptoms, they won't bother to come in for therapy. The problem with this approach is that it never gets to the root of the problem. It is like walking around on an injured leg and taking painkillers so that you can't feel it.

Sooner or later you will reap the negative effects of these drugs, if not in the form of physical side-effects, then at least in the form of unrealized potential to live life at its fullest. When you numb yourself, it is possible to do further injury without even realizing it. Instead of plugging your ears to the voice inside that tells you something is wrong, why not start spending time doing Anger Work and heal for good? Then you may be able to work towards throwing those drugs away.

There are some disorders that require medication. But even persons diagnosed with schizophrenia or manic depression, which have clear genetic components, need to reduce the stress in their lives. Stress only exacerbates mental disorders. People who suffer from these disorders can reduce stress in their lives, and thereby sometimes reduce their symptoms, by taking a three-mile walk each day. I have worked with several teenagers in my career who were on the edge of showing clear schizophrenic signs. By doing Anger Work and exercising daily, we were able to prevent the symptoms from ever fully developing.

How Long?

People often ask me how long they will need to do Anger Work to heal from the abuse and pain of their past. My response is that you must keep doing Anger Work about your past until you can tell that you are fully healed. The actual number of days, months, or years that it takes to arrive at this place varies from person to person depending on how severe the emotional wound is and how consistent you are about working on it.

You will know that you have reached this point when you can look at the event that has wounded you, and you no longer feel intense anger or sadness. The memory is clear, but it no longer has the power to evoke such strong emotions from you. Recalling the memory feels almost like going to a play or movie. Have you ever been to a movie or read a novel that is very tragic, and yet you walk away feeling only slightly moved? This is how you will eventually feel about your past.

I greatly enjoy William Shakespeare's plays, and in particular *Romeo and Juliet*. Whenever I watch this play, I am moved to tears, but only for a moment. If someone were to bring it up in conversation later, I would not be gripped with emotion in the same way I was during the performance. This is how you will feel when you are done with your Anger Work over a particular issue. The story may still be sad in its retelling, but your feelings will be brief and transitory.

It will be like a wound that has healed and left a scar. The scar does not hurt, and most of the time, you don't even notice that it's there. When you do think about it, you can remember the pain, though diminishingly so with time. The wound itself does not hurt any more. You no longer wince at the touch of it, or limp around, favoring that hurt appendage of your heart.

When you have finished processing the memories of your past and they no longer have power over you, you will still need to work at maintaining your health. This will mean dealing with the aggravating situations of everyday life and not letting them fester. You can address the situation as it arises by implementing the techniques listed in the section on "Anger Work Methods" under the heading "Anger Work When You're Not Alone."

I also recommend physical exercise on a regular basis, so that if something does come up, you can deal with it while you are working out. Sometimes little things happen to annoy you and you don't think much of it at the time, but then later you realize you are in a grumpy mood. Your exercise time provides a perfect opportunity for you to recall the incident briefly and get it out of your system. A regular routine exercise means that you never have to wait very long to heal. This is a great way to avoid building up emotional "leftovers."

Even when you aren't doing Anger Work, exercise is one of the most effective mood regulators there is. This is partly due to the endorphins (a naturally occurring anti-depressant chemical) that the body releases into your system when you exercise. Regular exercise helps to smooth out those valleys of depression and peaks of agitation. It is certainly the most natural and healthy anti-depressant.

Living a Lifestyle of Health

In addition to doing your Anger Work, there are some other things that you will want to do to attain and maintain your optimal health. Anger Work is just one component of an overall healthy lifestyle, though it is a very important one, and a good one to start with. I would like to discuss some of the other changes that you will want to make if you are determined to live a life of wholeness and health.

One of the most important abilities you must develop is knowing when to stick up for yourself, when to back down, and when to back off. This is referred to as keeping healthy boundaries. The term "boundaries" is used because it is all about understanding the borders or boundary lines that delineate where you begin and the other person ends. In other words, this means knowing what is your business and what is someone else's. Good boundaries are like good fences: they make it very clear when you are trespassing on someone else's territory and when someone else is trespassing on yours.

With all my emphasis on Anger Work and being nice to others, some of you may be thinking that I advocate becoming doormats who spend time doing Anger Work after others have wiped their feet on you. This is far from the truth. That would be an example of poor boundaries because you would be letting someone else "trespass" on you.

What I am proposing is simply that you remain kind as you hold your ground. Both Martin Luther King Jr. and Mahatma Gandhi were non-abusive people of great power. Far from being doormats, they earned worldwide respect and changed the course of history. They did not stoop to engaging in violence or abusive behavior, and yet they stood up for their rights. Well, you may not have any desire to change world history; however, standing up to your boss and not letting your family members push you around may sound very appealing.

So what do you do besides the Anger Work, and treating the person nicely, when you are angry with someone? The most important thing is to call attention to their behavior without being rude or cruel. For instance, if someone comments that you have gained weight since the last time they saw you, you could respond by saying "That wasn't a very nice thing to say." Tell mean people about their behavior. You may get an apology, or at least your comment may serve as a deterrent for that person when they feel like being rude to you again in the future. Children and animals are frequently abused because they don't defend themselves and they don't make the abuse public. Statements like, "That wasn't very nice," or "That hurt my feelings," or questions such as "Did you mean to hurt my feelings?" or "Why did you say that?" will call the person's attention to their abusive behavior and make them think twice about treating you that way.

One day I was driving my car out of a mall where I had never been before. As I was leaving, I noticed there was a sign that said, "Entrance only." There was room for two cars, but this was the entrance. As soon as I noticed the sign, a man drove in and started yelling and swearing at me, saying all kinds of negative comments that I don't care to repeat. I rolled down my car window and politely asked the man if he was a nice guy. He became all flustered and finally said "yes." Then I asked him, "Why are you treating me badly for making a mistake?" I wasn't mean, and I didn't provoke him to escalate the confrontation, but I wasn't just going to let him abuse me for making an honest mistake either. I simply drew his attention to his own behavior by asking the obvious. He didn't say a word after that; he just put his head down and drove away.

On another occasion I was making a phone call to clear up a question I had about my car insurance. The agent was being very rude, so I asked her nicely if she was having a bad day. She asked me what I meant. I told her that she was not being very nice to me and that I was unaware that I had done anything to offend her, so might she be having a bad day? She did not answer, but she treated me nicely the rest of the conversation.

It is very important to stand up for yourself. You have a right to set boundaries that don't allow others to abuse you. Saying to someone "I don't want to talk about it right now; you are too upset. Let's talk about it when you've had a chance to cool down" is setting a boundary. Sometimes people will not back down, so you may need to ask them to leave, or leave yourself. In extreme cases, when a person will not leave, or allow you to leave, you may even have to involve the police. Be especially careful with people who are drinking or doing drugs. They lose impulse control and will do things that are unconscionable to a sober person. Don't hang out at clubs/bars or spend time with people who use substances to excess. If your spouse is a substance abuser, leave or call the police when he or she starts acting out. Rarely are you in a situation where you have no options, unless you are a child or in prison. Even in these situations, you can always do Anger Work.

Another part of setting good boundaries for yourself is trying to find jobs, friendships, and marriages in which people are positive, supportive, and treat you with respect. I strongly encourage you to find one or two friends who are particularly kind, loving, and gracious towards you. This may include a "significant other." Experiencing acceptance and unconditional love from someone who is aware of all your bad behavior is the most powerful healing agent that exists. Though no human being is capable of flawless love it is possible to build relationships that offer a wealth of forgiveness, understanding, and acceptance.

Think about having a friend or two who cares for you this much, and work at getting one. Finding friends of this caliber is a difficult and lengthy process, but well worth the effort. Creating contexts in which you can practice the giving and receiving of love and grace with others is truly one of life's richest experiences. If you can accomplish this in your own family, it only amplifies the experience.

If you do not have the support that you need to go through your healing process, it would be good to start working with a psychologist who is able to love you unconditionally. Find a therapist who won't shame you. This friend can support you and give you some guidance as you take the brave step of working through your current issues and memories from the past. Your therapist may not be familiar with the concept of Anger Work, but it will make sense when you explain it. Enlist the person's support and do your Anger Work.

When looking for prospective friends and mates, remember that the best predictor of how someone will treat you is not necessarily how they are currently treating you. Rather, it is how that person treats her/himself and how s/he has treated others who have been close to her/him. Many people can stay on their best behavior for a while, but don't expect anyone who is abusive to his mom, ex-boyfriend, child, or ex-wife to treat you totally differently just because you're a different person. How we treat others has more to do with ourselves than it does with the people in our lives.

Some people are very gracious toward everyone except their spouses, their children, or their significant others. A friend of mine has an explanation she calls the Bubble Theory for why some people, as the old song says, "only hurt the ones they love." It goes like this: everyone is surrounded by an invisible bubble. This bubble marks the boundary between oneself and the outside world. We are very selective about whom we let inside the bubble. Usually it includes yourself, significant others, and your children.

The people inside of the bubble are sometimes viewed as extensions of or appendages to the self . . . my wife, my husband, my kid; therefore they are treated however that individual treats him or herself. If a person is loving and gracious to oneself, then this poses no problem. When a person is harshly self-critical and self-demanding, those close to her or him can expect to be shown the same meager amounts of grace by that person.

For example, some people are fastidious about their own housekeeping but don't care when other peoples' homes are messy because it isn't their home. But if they have a family member living in the same household who doesn't share their neat tendencies, the same grace is not extended. I've seen some families in which "Clean your room!" becomes the battle cry of a civil war, which nearly tears the family asunder. When *mi casa es tú casa* (In other words when you live under the same roof), it's a whole different story.

Another example is a quiet coworker who is so passive and seems so timid at work. Then one day you see the police come and take her away for child abuse of her six-year-old son. How could such a timid person abuse her own child? Because inside she loathes herself and when her children are born, she treats them just as she treats herself. If you ever get as close to one of these people as their spouse or children are, you will need to be careful.

As you search for a soul mate or a good friend to "hang out" with, pay attention to how people treat themselves and those inside their bubble. Sooner or later this is how they will treat you, if you get close enough. Choose people who are kind to others, who won't "blast" you when you make a mistake, for you *will* make mistakes. The way a person treats you when you do something wrong is a good indicator of his or her true self. Once you find some good people, give those relationships your time and energy. Love them and treat them well, for they will probably not put up with your abuse, just as you do not want to put up with the abuse of others.

Another thing to be cautious of when forming relationships is people who like to do a lot of teasing. Usually teasing is at the expense of another person, and it generally has some underlying truth and hostility connected with it. Teasing is a bad habit that tears people down rather than building them up. As the old adage goes, "With friends like that, who needs enemies?"

You will probably want to talk to people who are already in your life about the importance of being kind during confrontations. You may want to set some rules that you can both agree to follow while discussing disagreements, such as no name-calling, etc. Make the boundaries clear. Then if a difficult issue comes up, it will be easier to discuss it respectfully.

If you find that there are certain people in your life who are consistently abusive and who do not respond well to your attempts to set healthy boundaries, then you need to work toward getting these people out of your life. Most people have some abusers in their lives who don't need to be there. For example, if you buy your groceries at a market where the clerk is regularly rude to you, then try to shop somewhere else. If you boss is an abusive person, see if you can transfer or find a new job. This will be better than putting up with abuse day after day.

The two changes involved in setting healthy boundaries that have the greatest impact for many of my clients are: to change jobs, or to end a relationship with an abusive significant other. I know that for some of you, this may not be an option, but for the rest of you, the impact of getting hurtful people out of your life can be immense.

Sally was a high school teacher who loved her job, at least she had loved it for the first eight years. The problem was that her principal had a very negative attitude. He was regularly making Sally's job unpleasant by criticizing her teaching methods and by discounting every idea that Sally proposed during staff meetings. Sally couldn't stand her boss, and her life had become fraught with stress. She had to keep her emotional guard up every minute or she would be bowled over by another one of his cruel and disrespectful comments. She tried to confront him once, but he told her she was just being overly sensitive.

When Sally came to me, she hated her job and reported to me that she felt like "a nervous wreck" all the time. Her self-esteem had eroded considerably over the last few years, and she was wondering if she had chosen the wrong profession. She knew that her principal was a "real jerk," but she didn't realize that he was a large part of her problem.

I encouraged Sally to transfer to a new school and see if having a principal with a positive attitude made a difference. She did that. Her new school had a wonderfully positive principal who was supportive of Sally's creative approach to problem solving and slightly unconventional teaching methods. By the third month of her new job, Sally found that she looked forward to going to work each day. She had recaptured the joy of teaching and vowed with determination that she would never let anyone cause her to doubt her teaching ability again.

Supervisors can vary greatly in personality and style of management. You can't expect to see eye to eye with your boss on every issue; however, if your relationship with your boss has become adversarial, and there is nothing you can do to remedy the situation, it may be time to start looking for a new job. You spend too much of your life at work to put up with that kind of stress and unhappiness.

Many people stay in abusive marriages because of their children. I would encourage you to think about two things. First, what impact is your staying going to have on your children if you or your spouse is verbally or emotionally abusing your children because of the tension in the house? Second, even if your children aren't being abused, what are you modeling for them?

Look to see how much your own marriage is like that of your parents. Often that which you swore you would never do when you got older becomes a reality. This is because of the power of modeling. If you don't do Anger Work on the poor modeling you received and then work hard toward changing it, you will repeat the same patterns. Chances are that your children will end up in a relationship to whatever you model for them. Is that what you want? Modeling affects your children as much as how you treat them does. The longer I work with children, the more I see this. If you are modeling a bad marriage, I would encourage you to work towards healing your marriage if at all possible. If this cannot be done, then you should consider separating and moving ahead.

One brave woman I knew would not divorce her abusive husband because of her religious beliefs, but she was willing to live separately from him for three years. During this long separation, her husband was able to see the error of his ways and repent. She allowed him to move back in and now he treats her nicely. However, if he ever reverts back to his abusive ways, he will be told to leave again for as long as it takes him to learn to treat her with kindness and respect her boundaries.

Not all of the components of a healthy lifestyle are as difficult to achieve as healthy boundaries. One of the easiest and most basic changes you can make to improve your outlook on life is to build the right amount of sleep that you need and then get it every night. Adequate sleep, like exercise, is another helpful tool in regulating your moods. Most adults need an average of eight hours per night. This is a good guideline, but you may find that you function best with seven-and-one-half or nine. If you think that you do fine with four or five hours or that you need twelve hours of sleep per night, I would encourage you to reevaluate. If you haven't started doing Anger Work yet, start and see if that makes any difference.

In addition to this, learn about healthy eating. Eating right not only feeds the body, but feeds the soul with the reassuring knowledge that you are taking good care of yourself. Feeding your body well is like getting routine maintenance done on your car: it helps it to run better and last longer.

Another habit you will want to form is learning to play regularly. This can be challenging for a lot of people to learn to do, but the process is quite . . . well, fun! This doesn't mean that you have to whip out the Play-doh and Silly String if that's not your style. It means that you need to have numerous aspects of your life that are pure pleasure, like watching sunsets a few times a week, or exchanging massages with a good friend. Your playing might take the form of taking long baths, or art classes, or walks along the beach.

Something else you might want to work on is limiting the negative input into your life. Everything we watch or listen to gets stored somewhere in our minds, and in that sense it becomes a part of us. For this reason I encourage you to become more aware of the lyrics that you listen to on the radio. Even when you aren't giving the music your full attention, it is still making its way into your mind. Just think about how some people listen to audio cassettes while they sleep as a form of self-hypnosis to help them lose weight or quit smoking. If those messages can make their way in, then so can song lyrics. What are you feeding to your subconscious mind?

Likewise, consider the violence portrayed in many movies and television programs. How good can it be for you to watch women being raped and brutalized? Or to see those frightening "psycho" type looks on the faces of characters just before they commit homicide? How about those soap-operas sirens who somehow manage to manipulate the lives of every other character in the script? And those popular sit-coms in which you can sit and listen to a husband and wife or a couple of friends rag on each other for an entire thirty minutes or more? What are you feeding your soul?

Watching or reading filmed biographies or novels about people who have triumphed against the odds can lift the human spirit and inspire you with newfound motivation. If a positive book or movie can have that much impact for the good, we need to ask the obvious question, what power might a disturbing one have?

Healthy, young children, provide a good model of sensitivity.

When I am working with children, they frequently tell me about movies they have seen. I don't bring up the topic; they just want to tell me about some movie or TV show that disturbed them and then they do Anger Work. If something is that disturbing to a child, then it is often not good for adults either. If we do not find it disturbing, it may be that we have just allowed ourselves to become desensitized. Perhaps we should follow the lead of the children and spend an evening snuggled in bed reading A.A. Milne's *Winnie the Pooh* instead of watching another violent movie.

Our goal as self-actualizing human beings is to achieve a well-rounded, healthy lifestyle. One that is not only empty of repressed emotion, but also <u>full</u> of joy, peace, and meaningful relationships. In order to accomplish this goal, we need to recognize that Anger Work is only one important element of a larger set of practices that will bring us to this place. Some of the other habits we need to develop include: sticking up for ourselves; getting abusive people out of our lives and surrounding ourselves with kind people; getting enough sleep; eating well; playing often; and limiting the negative input into our lives. As you continue on your path to wholeness, I'm sure you will find that incorporating these practices will bring a new depth and richness to your life.

What to Do When You've Really Messed Up

Letting go of shame is very hard, I have experienced this in my own life. When I was in my own therapy, as part of my training to become a psychologist, one of the worst things that I had to face was what I had done to my two cats. After finishing my first four years of college, I was unable to take care of my two cats. I was moving to live on campus at new university where pets were not permitted. My parents were unable to take care of my cats for me any longer because they too were moving. I had two choices: I could take my cats to the pound and put them to sleep or I could find a home for them. (There was no animal shelter available at that time.)

I couldn't find anyone who would take them, but I couldn't bear to take them to the pound, so I drove with them into the country to find just the right farm. My tears flowed as one of the cats sat on my lap. Although the season was summer, I knew that this region had harsh winters. Nevertheless, in my despair, I put both cats out on the driveway of the farm. I did not go to the farmers and ask them if they would keep the cats; I just left them. One cat took off into the woods and the other just stood on the road looking at me. Both cats had been declawed and had been indoor cats all their lives. I knew that their chances of survival were very slim. This is one of the worst things that I have ever done, and to this day, I cannot think about it without feeling some sadness. There have been other harmful things that I have done, but never again to innocent and defenseless animals.

I have talked to many people about what I did. I have repeatedly asked God and my cats to forgive me, and I know that I am forgiven. But I am still sad over what I did, even after twenty years. There is no way that I can make it up to those two cats, but as a sort of penance, and a way to help myself heal, I always visit cats that I see outdoors and give them some of my love. Doing this makes me feel better because I know that I am doing something of the opposite nature of the mistake that I made earlier. Without trying to get too philosophical, it is like giving something back to the universe that I took away at an earlier date. It does nothing to help my two cats, but it makes me feel at harmony again.

Of course, there are going to be things that you have done that are going to be hard to forgive yourself for. Others will forgive you more easily than you will forgive yourself. When you discover these areas, the first thing you want to do is ask yourself if there is anything that you can do to directly make up for your mistakes. For example, when I was in third grade, I had broken the pencil of a friend of mine while I was teasing him. He got very upset and cried. I felt so bad that the next day I gave him about twenty pencils, and for the next month, I gave him a pencil a day. My friend knew that I was genuinely sorry for what I had done. He forgave me, which helped me to forgive myself. Our friendship was mended and I learned a lesson. No permanent damage was done. Making up for your mistakes when possible can really be worth it, no matter how costly.

When I work with parents of grown children who do not want to have anything to do with them, I encourage the parent to send notes of love and encouragement several times a month, all their lives. Even if there is no change in the relationship, at least my clients are giving unconditional love and they can look in the mirror with respect. Love your children, do not criticize them. Of course, do your Anger Work, but love them.

If the person whom you hurt is now out of your life, you may want to try to find that person and write him or her a letter. This could take some time and energy, but the shame is more costly. Apologize and ask for forgiveness in your letter. If the person chooses to respond, you will usually find that what you did was not as life-altering for them as you thought. Finding that out can be a great release. Even if the person really was as negatively affected as you feared, at least you can live the rest of your life knowing that you tried to make amends.

There are some situations in which this is not possible or not advisable. You may have killed someone or done someone such harm that to be contacted by you would be frightening for that person. If someone has made efforts to hide their whereabouts from you, then you need to respect their boundary and let them have their space. In that case, I recommend that you confess what you have done to at least one other person so that you can experience some release. (Choose someone who will not judge and shame you, perhaps a priest, rabbi, sponsor, or psychologist.)

You may also want to design some sort of ceremony for yourself to give yourself the release of confessing and asking forgiveness from that person. This might take the form of writing a letter to the person and then putting it in a bottle in the ocean, or watching it burn in your fireplace while you concentrate on the feeling that as the smoke rises it carries your feelings out upon the wind and to that person. You may want to work with your therapist and do a role-play of yourself apologizing to the person. Be creative and do whatever you feel will help you release your sense of shame.

This is not about going into denial that what you did was wrong; this is about acknowledging that fact, and getting beyond it. You are refusing to give that mistake the power to decide what kind of person you are. It wants you to be a bad person with a miserable life, but you can choose to be a good person who made a bad decision and then learned from it.

After you have done this, even though you can't make amends with the original person whom you hurt, ask yourself if there is something you can do to help make up for your mistake. While I don't think that God needs us to do penance in order to forgive us, I think it can be very helpful in the process of forgiving ourselves. In the movie *Gandhi,* a man approaches Gandhi and confesses to having killed the baby of his enemy. Instead of shaming the man, Gandhi exhorts him to find a orphan child of his enemy's kind and raise it in the religious ways of his enemy.

In an extreme case, for example if you are truly responsible for destroying the life of one or more human beings, you may want to give your life to some mission or cause that takes most of your time, such as loving and serving the poor. If this keeps you from the shame and helps you heal, what greater life could you hope for?

Find a way to forgive yourself for your own bad behavior. You may want to seek spiritual guidance to help you learn how to do this. If there are days when your love for yourself is not enough to make you want to heal, remember that the self-destruct method is costly to others as well. Shame puts very bad thoughts about yourself into your head, and with time, you will probably act on them. You will hurt a lot more people in your life as shame drives you to live up to that negative self-concept.

Another thing that you can do to help yourself heal is Anger Work. If you have done some really raunchy things in your life, try to trace the path of how you got to that point. Recall the various negative influences and choices in your life. Do Anger Work focused on each of these that you remember. I'm not suggesting that you abdicate responsibility for your behavior, but allow yourself to get really "pissed off" that those influences were in your life and be angry that you took such wrong turns.

Be careful not to fall into saying "I'm so stupid" or calling yourself names while you're doing your Anger Work. Remember that shaming yourself will only encourage you to do more evil. Instead, tell yourself "I am <u>so</u> angry that I made the choice I did. I wish I had seen more clearly and had not gone down that path.

Thank God I can see it now and can change." Every time you hit the punching bag, you are hitting that decision or that former way of thinking and "kicking its butt" so to speak. Don't give your past mistakes any more power over you. That's not who you want to be. Use your anger to give you the energy to change.

In light of how hard it is to forgive yourself when you really mess up, you are going to want to make sure that you avoid adding anything to the load you are already working on. It is especially important for you to remember the two keys to successful Anger Work: 1. No taking-out our anger on yourself, and 2. No taking-out your anger on others (including animals).

This includes people who are abusive. Don't let them abuse you, but don't abuse them back if they do. Let life bring them justice. They will reap what they sow; life is very just in that way. Just as you bear the burden of the mistakes you've made, so will they have to carry with them the knowledge of whatever they have done or tried to do to you. You will find that the more you do your Anger Work, the less you will wish for them to suffer. They will still suffer, but you will come to a place where you wish them well.

Conclusion

In conclusion I would like to review the main points that I hope you will take with you and apply in your own life after having read this book.

Everyone has situations and experiences in life that are the source of suffering and aggravation. There are only two emotions that we can use to respond to these situations that will bring about healing for us and bring us back to an emotional equilibrium. These two emotions are anger and sadness. This truth is easy to observe by watching children who either cry or get angry in response to things that upset them.

If we fail to express our anger or sadness about what has happened to us, then these emotions will not go away. Rather, they will accumulate and will eventually manifest themselves in the form of depression, stress-related illness, compulsive behavior, or some form of addiction.

Some addictions, such as workaholism, or busyism (the addiction to other meaningful activities such as charity work, religious activities, or carting your children to every possible team and club), can be very subtle, and are often applauded by others. Though the activities may be good in and of themselves, when you use them to avoid our feelings about the emotional issues in your life, they have become an addiction for you.

Ultimately, the habit of consistently making activity a higher priority than self-reflection or dealing with the tougher issues of life, will make you a shallow person. At best, you will not live up to your full potential. At worst, you will stumble through life leaving casualties in your path, people whom you hurt because you were too busy to take the time to really think about what you were doing.

Anger and sadness are the two emotions that we can utilize to process life's negative experiences and flush out the unwanted residual effects of them. The problem with using sadness as the primary mode of healing is that many people slip right into depression when they try to practice sadness. Depression is in no way beneficial. However, many people have a hard time distinguishing the difference, or directing themselves away from depression and into healthy sadness. As a result they can get caught in a slump for long periods of time without making any progress. It is for this reason that I generally, though not exclusively, recommend that my clients focus on their anger over their sadness as they process the traumatic experiences of their past.

Anger Work is a tool that can be utilized by anyone to help maintain his or her own emotional health. It is a technique that involves focusing on the negative event while expressing anger about it. For people who have had no major tragedies or abuse in their lives, Anger Work can be used to release the stress of everyday life, which can sometimes lead to grumpy moods, depression, overeating, or destructive arguments. For people who have experienced severe loss or abuse in their lives, Anger Work can be used to process those experiences, and free themselves from the negative effects of those traumas.

There are two essential keys to successful Anger Work. The first one is that you must not take out your anger on yourself. The primary reason for this is that the more you tell yourself how horrible you are, and make yourself feel like the scum of the earth, the more you will internalize that image of yourself. The more you see yourself that way, the more you will act that part. The whole point of Anger Work is to disentangle you from the grip of the past and free you to live a full and happy life. Berating yourself works in the exact opposite direction to counteract the Anger Work that you are doing and make it unsuccessful.

The second essential key to successful Anger Work is that you must not take out your anger on others, including animals. While there are many good reasons to follow this guideline, the reason that it is so essential to successful Anger Work is that each time you knowingly hurt another, you add to the accumulation of sludge that you then have to work through.

I ask you to recall the analogy that compares the unresolved emotional issues in your life with a pool of stagnant water. In order for you to clear that area so that the grass can grow (i.e., you can feel happy and complete), you need to somehow clear out that murky water. Anger Work is successful when it serves to bail out that water for you. You are never going to make any significant headway if each pan of fetid water that you bail out is replaced by some equally slimy source of shame that you have created by choosing to abuse others. Each time you act abusively, you extend the time you will need to work through your issues and come to a place of peace.

In the chapter on "Anger Work Methods," I listed many different techniques that you can use to express your anger while focusing on whatever hurt you or made you angry. Most of these techniques involve some sort of physical exertion or exercise. This is because I believe that it works best when the body, mind, and spirit are all involved in the healing of the whole person. I have found that clients who incorporate some form of movement into their Anger Work routines improve more rapidly.

There is a great deal of room for creativity when it comes to the actual details of how you carry out your Anger Work. The techniques listed are only suggestions that have worked for other people. They are there to help you get started. Once you've tried a few of them, you will start to get a feel for what works for you and what doesn't. I encourage you to tailor your routines to your own personality. You may find that your preferences change over the course of time, or depending on what issue you are working on. This is natural.

When you get ready to do your Anger Work, choose a location that allows you as much privacy as you need. This way you will not subject yourself to unnecessary negative feedback from others. You will also avoid frightening or confusing any family members or others who may not understand what you are doing.

Allow yourself to ease into doing Anger Work. This will build your trust in yourself and your confidence in using Anger Work techniques. Don't be alarmed if you find yourself moving in cycles in which you are more "into" your Anger Work, followed by periods in which you are less engaged. This is part of the natural ebb and flow of emotions.

The techniques of Anger work provide you with the opportunity to transform your life. By doing Anger Work, you can improve the relationships in your life and your own feelings about yourself. Anger Work is a tool that you can keep in your back pocket and use to handle whatever life throws your way, from minor annoyances to major tragedies with an astounding level of emotional stability.

As with anything of real value, there is a cost involved. The cost of obtaining the benefits that Anger Work has to offer you come in the form of time and personal energy. You will need to spend a fair amount of each doing Anger Work to process your feelings about the negative experiences of your life. Exactly how much time depends on the particular wounds that you need to heal, and how much you apply yourself. Your emotional wellness will need to be a top priority. This will probably mean paring down some of the unessential activities in your life to make time for the essential: self-reflection and becoming the person you were intended to be.

The time and energy that it takes to commit yourself to healing through Anger Work may seem like a lot to ask, but I assure you that it is nothing compared to the price you will eventually pay if you choose to ignore your repressed feelings and unresolved emotional issues. This kind of self-neglect often leads people into depression, ruptured relationships, stress-related illness, compulsive or addictive behavior, and a host of other psychological problems.

Although Anger Work is not the only thing you need to learn to live an emotionally healthy and fulfilling life, it is a large piece of the puzzle. It is something you can do right away that will give you noticeable results. Still, it is important to work on developing the other habits of healthy living discussed in this book. These will be woven together to form the strong fabric of a life of wholeness and wellness.

My best wishes and hopes go with you on your journey to wholeness. May you experience the cleansing power of Anger Work as you stomp your way down the path of healing. And some day soon, may you experience the joy and aliveness that rush in to replace all those feelings you kept bottled up for so long.

If you are interested in seeing Dr. Puff as a client for psychotherapy, would like to attend one of his seminars on Anger Work, or would like to book a lecture or seminar series on Anger Work for your business or organization, please call or write the address below for more information:

Dr. Robert Puff
749 So. Brea Blvd., Suite 42
Brea, CA 92821
(714) 491-PUFF

Please note, Southern California is regularly changing their area codes, so if this number does not work, please call directory assistance and ask for Dr. Puff's office in Brea, California.